by Rob Willson and Rhena Branch

A John Wiley and Sons, Ltd, Publication

CBT Journal For Dummies®

Published by
John Wiley & Sons, Ltd
The Atrium
Southern Gate
Chichester
West Sussex
PO19 8SQ
England

Email (for orders and customer service enquires): cs-books@wiley.co.uk

Visit our home page on www.wiley.com

For general information on our other products and services, please contact our Customer Care Department within the U.S. at 877-762-2974, outside the U.S. at 317-572-3993, or fax 317-572-4002.

For technical support, please visit www.wiley.com/techsupport.

Wiley also publishes its books in a variety of electronic formats and by print-on-demand. Some content that appears in standard print versions of this book may not be available in other formats. For more information about Wiley products, visit us at www.wiley.com.

ISBN 978-1-119-97535-9 (pbk)

Printed in the UK by TJ International Ltd., Padstow, Cornwall.

10 9 8 7 6 5 4 3 2 1

WILEY

About the Authors

Rob Willson, BSc, MSc, Dip SBHS, currently divides the majority of his work time between private practice and conducting research on Body Dysmorphic Disorder at the Institute of Psychiatry, London. Previously he spent twelve years working at the Priory Hospital, North London where he was a therapist and therapy services manager. He also trained numerous CBT therapists over a seven-year period at Goldsmith's College, University of London. Rob's main clinical interests are anxiety and obsessional problems, and disseminating CBT principles through self-help. He has made several TV appearances including in the BBC documentary 'Too Ugly for Love'.

Rhena Branch, MSc, Dip CBT, is an accredited CBT therapist and holds a post-graduate clinical supervision qualification. Rhena runs a private practice with offices in North and Central London. She also teaches and supervises on the MSc course in CBT/REBT at Goldsmith's College, University of London. Rhena treats general psychiatric disorders and has a special interest in eating disorders.

Dedication

For Felix and Atticus (from Rhena)

For Emma and Lucy (from Rob)

Authors' Acknowledgments

From both of us: Many researchers, fellow therapists and authors have influenced our understanding and practice of CBT over the years and therefore the content in this book. Founding fathers, Albert Ellis and Aaron T. Beck, of course merit special mention. Others include (in no specific order): Ray DiGiuseppe, Mary-Anne Layden, Jacqueline Persons, David A. Clarke, Adrian Wells, Stanley Rachman, Paul Salkovskis, Christine Padesky, Michael Neenan, David Veale, David M. Clark, David Burns, Kevin Gournay and many more. Special thanks goes to Windy Dryden for his extensive writings and for teaching us both so much.

Finally, a genuine thank you to all our clients (past and present) for allowing us to get to know you and learn from you.

Publisher's Acknowledgments

We're proud of this book; please send us your comments at http://dummies.custhelp.com. For other comments, please contact our Customer Care Department within the U.S. at 877-762-2974, outside the U.S. at 317-572-3993, or fax 317-572-4002.

Some of the people who helped bring this book to market include the following:

Acquisitions, Editorial, and Vertical Websites

Project Editor: Simon Bell

Acquisitions Editor: Kerry Laundon

Assistant Editor: Ben Kemble

Technical Editor: David Knight

Production Manager: Daniel Mersey

Publisher: David Palmer

Cartoons: Rich Tennant
(www.the5thwave.com)

Composition Services

Project Coordinator: Kristie Rees

Layout and Graphics: Mark Pinto, Erin Zeltner

Proofreader: Laura Albert

Publishing and Editorial for Consumer Dummies

    Kathleen Nebenhaus, Vice President and Executive Publisher

    Kristin Ferguson-Wagstaffe, Product Development Director

    Ensley Eikenburg, Associate Publisher, Travel

    Kelly Regan, Editorial Director, Travel

Publishing for Technology Dummies

    Andy Cummings, Vice President and Publisher

Composition Services

    Debbie Stailey, Director of Composition Services

Contents at a Glance

Table of Contents

Introduction

● ●

*C*ognitive behavioural therapy, or CBT, is growing in popularity as an efficient and long-lasting treatment for many different types of psychological problem.

In addition, whether you think your problems are minimal, you're living the life of Riley, you feel mildly depressed, or you've had years of uncomfortable psychological symptoms, CBT can help you. Because of its practical and educational nature CBT especially lends itself to self-help material and has provided help in this way for many years. The range and quality of CBT self-help material continues to grow, and we hope this book will act as a companion to you in your journey towards fuller emotional health.

About This Book

This book is designed to help you set aside twelve weeks to improving your emotional health. Clearly we don't expect the whole of each of those weeks to be given over to improving your happiness (although from time to time your mind might deserve a working day's worth of rehabilitation).

You are most likely to be using this book as a companion to self-help or professional CBT (which as it happens, almost always relies heavily on self-help called 'home-work'). As you go through the twelve weeks you'll be introduced to a number of CBT-based exercises and techniques. These may be appropriate to the specific stage in personal change you are at, or might be something to come back to. In any case they are designed to stimulate your own 'self-therapist' mind and to help to keep you going in a healthy and helpful direction.

Conventions Used in This Book

To make your reading experience easier and to alert you to key words or points, we use certain conventions.

- ✔ *Italics* introduce new terms, underscore key differences in meaning between words, and highlight the most important aspects of a sentence or example.

- ✔ Where appropriate, we use the terms 'him' in even-numbered chapters and 'her' in odd-numbered chapters when writing, with a view to incorporating gender equality.

Foolish Assumptions

In writing this little tome, we make the following assumptions about you, dear reader:

- ✔ You're human.

- ✔ As a human, you're likely at some stage in your life to experience some sort of emotional problem that you'd like to surmount.

✔ You've heard about CBT, or are intrigued by CBT, or have had CBT suggested to you by a doctor, friend, or mental health professional as a possible treatment for your specific difficulties.

✔ Even if you don't think you're particularly in need of CBT right now, you want to discover more about some of the principles outlined in this book.

✔ You think that your life is absolutely fine right now, but you want to find interesting and useful information in the book that will enhance your life further.

✔ You're keen to find out whether CBT may be helpful to someone close to you.

How This Book Is Organised

This book is divided into four main sections. Part I is a brief introduction to CBT. Part II is filled with twelve weeks worth of CBT-based guidance, principles, techniques and exercises. There is also space for you to record your progress as you go. There is also enough free space for you to add your own collection of thoughts, images, inspirational quotes, records of your self-help and anything else relevant to your CBT. Part III covers things to consider next once you have completed your twelve weeks. Part IV, as in every *For Dummies* book, is a Part of Tens.

Icons Used in This Book

We use the following icons in this book to alert you to certain types of information that you can choose to read, commit to memory (and possibly interject into dinner party conversation), or maybe just utterly ignore:

This icon is a cheerful, if sometimes urgent, reminder of important points to take notice of.

When you see this icon it's over to you to write down your thoughts and feelings on your CBT journey – and whatever else occurs to you – in the space provided.

Use the space which follows this icon to record responses to the lead-in text on the preceding page.

Part I
Introducing CBT Journal

The 5th Wave   By Rich Tennant

"I'm making up a list of my problems. The first one is a fear of making lists."

In this part . . .

*Y*ou'll get to grips with what CBT stands for and how it can help you. If you're a newcomer to the world of CBT, this is a useful overview of what CBT is and what you can use it for. If you're familiar with CBT practice, through *CBT For Dummies,* say, think of this part as a timely refresher.

Introducing the CBT Journal

- -

In This Chapter

▶ A brief introduction to what CBT is all about

▶ The purpose of keeping a journal

▶ Using this book to help you make the most of CBT

- -

*T*his book's chief aim is to be your companion in using cognitive behavioural therapy (CBT) to help improve your emotional and psychological well-being. What follows is a short introduction (or refresher course for some readers) to the basics of cognitive behavioural therapy. We also outline the merits of keeping a journal, especially alongside using the principles and techniques of CBT.

CBT: A Brief Introduction

CBT is an approach to psychological therapy that is most strongly associated with helping people change the way they think and behave. CBT practitioners see emotions as interconnected with thoughts and behaviours, so it follows that if these thoughts and behaviours are targeted for change, a change in emotions will result. CBT therapists over the years have been told 'it's a lot more complicated than that!' by a great many psychotherapists, biologists, neurologists, geneticists and sociologists (we could go on). To their criticism we say 'Er, yes of course it is . . . it's just that we're mostly focused on keeping the process simple enough that people can use it. Oh, and by the way, have you seen all the research studies that show how effective CBT is?'

Of course our biology, genetics, personal history, environment, and brain influence how we feel, think, and act. Thankfully we don't need to change all of those elements to give our emotional health a serious lift. Your beliefs, thoughts (and how you relate to them), mental activities, and behaviour all have a powerful effect on your emotions, especially when you combine them as a shift in attitude or *mode* (a connected pattern of thoughts, feeling and behaviour).

The cognitive behavioural therapies

One of the more reasonable questions asked of CBT therapists is 'What exactly is CBT?' The founding father of CBT, Aaron T. Beck, famously used to answer 'anything that works!' or 'anything that helps get the patient from problem to goal'. As psychological therapy grows as a field, these broad definitions seem in some ways more apt than ever. CBT is very much a 'school of therapies' rather than a single approach, and some of these therapies overlap considerably. Here are some of the current 'types' of CBT, in no special order:

- ✔ **Behaviour therapy (BT):** Most often associated with 'exposure', the therapeutic use of facing your fears. Another key contribution is to understand the *function* and consequences of our behaviour in the context of emotional problems.

- ✔ **Cognitive therapy (CT):** Founded by Aaron T. Beck, and using thought diaries and behavioural experiments, CT focuses upon uncovering unhelpful thoughts, rules and assumptions or beliefs, aiming to replace them with more helpful alternatives.

- **Rational emotive behaviour therapy (REBT):** Developed by Albert Ellis, REBT is philosophical, promoting flexible thinking, high frustration tolerance, and self-acceptance. Behaviour change is seen as acting upon, and therefore strengthening, healthy beliefs.

- **Acceptance and commitment therapy (ACT):** Conceived by Steven Hayes, ACT tends to focus more upon acceptance of your current reactions, mindfulness of the present moment, identifying your valued directions (what you're really 'about' as a person) and committed action.

- **Mindfulness-based cognitive therapy (MBCT):** The founders of this perspective are Jon Kabat-Zinn, Zindel Segal, Mark Williams, and John Teasdale. MBCT is a blend of CT with mindfulness techniques associated with Buddhism. MBCT can involve mindfulness meditation practice, alongside learning to practise detached, non-judgmental, observation of events and one's inner reactions to them.

- **Metacognitive therapy (MCT):** MCT was founded by Adrian Wells and Gerald Matthews. MCT focuses upon the thoughts we have *about* our mental processes, such as dwelling on the past, focusing on future threats, confidence in our memory, and where we focus our attention. MCT also tackles practices that are 'backfiring' as coping strategies and which therefore keep the problem going.

- **Compassionate mind training (CMT):** Developed by Paul Gilbert, CMT focuses upon the importance of shame and self-criticism in emotional problems. It encourages people to become warmer and more compassionate to themselves by using a variety of imagery, and attention and behavioural strategies.

- **Behavioural activation (BA):** Most often associated with Christopher Martell, BA is a treatment for depression. BA helps patients 'activate' themselves out of the patterns of inactivity and avoidance driven by depression. The key is that the patterns targeted are those that will increase the person's reward and range of activities, or at least make the person's environment less unpleasant.

Using what works

In this and our other books based on CBT techniques and principles, we try to bring you some of the techniques from these various CBT approaches that we've found to be most useful in real-world clinical practice. Many of the techniques don't belong to a particular approach, not least because so many of them draw from the same pool of literature, conferences, training and studies, but also because many approaches are extensions and developments of earlier approaches. Crucially a good CBT approach (and CBT therapist) will help you feel like you understand your problem better, and that you have a clearer idea of what you need to do in order to overcome it. We've also drawn from other research on mental health and happiness, such as Martin Seligman's work on *positive psychology*, where there's evidence that it can further assist your growth and recovery.

Keeping the CBT Journal

This is (as far as we know) a unique book. It offers a mix of advice and techniques alongside free space in which to keep your own personal journal.

The inspiration for this journal has been the numerous people we've seen for therapy who take notes and keep a record of things they have learned from their CBT. Our observation is that people who take notes on what they have learned tend to make their recovery more efficiently. Furthermore, 'expressive writing' has been shown in research to help people improve emotional problems.

Our hope is that you will be able to relate material that you generate during emotionally focused writing to your CBT. Writing down your thoughts and feelings each day on your road to recovery can help you get better all the faster.

Assessing your actions

We're including in this section the way you do things in your head, since mental activities can be just as powerful as behavioural activities in driving your emotional problems. A critical phrase to bear in mind when you're establishing what's keeping your problem going is *the solution is the problem.* This means that the strategies you are using to cope with your existing emotional problem may very well be what are keeping it going. (These strategies are sometimes referred to as *safety behaviours.*)

In particular, the kinds of strategies that may be causing you problems are those aimed at controlling or avoiding your emotions, thoughts or bodily sensations. Your mind is very much like your body in that it makes good sense to take care of it and keep it in overall good shape, and to allow it to carry out most of its key functions on autopilot. Just as you don't try to control the blood that flows through your veins, you may need to check that you're not over-controlling your mind and emotional system.

The kinds of strategies you may be using to cope with problems include:

- Avoiding situations that trigger anxiety

- Withdrawing and isolating yourself

- Compulsions (for example to check, clean, or wash)

- Dwelling upon and reviewing past events

- Repeatedly seeking reassurance

- Criticising yourself or others in your mind

- Comparing yourself with other people

- Analysing what people have said to you

- Reviewing interactions with other people

- Using alcohol or non-prescribed drugs as a 'treatment' for your problems

- Over-planning and preparing for future events in your mind

Other more subtle safety behaviours include:

- Gripping a cup tightly to try to stop people seeing you shake (in social phobia)

- Holding onto something for fear of collapse due to anxiety (in panic with agoraphobia)

- Avoiding bright lighting (in body dysmorphic disorder)

These lists are by no means exhaustive. If your mood has become low, you may also notice that you have become less good at looking after your home, have neglected your personal grooming, have changed your eating patterns, or have irregular sleep patterns.

One of the ways to identify potentially unhelpful strategies is to imagine waking up tomorrow morning to find that your emotional problems have completely gone and you feel considerably better. Now consider how you might feel, think, and act differently. Later in this book we'll give you the opportunity to write down some of the strategies that are connected to the maintenance of your problems.

Writing and recording

CBT combines four main factors:

- ✔ Gaining a new perspective on your emotions
- ✔ Rehabilitating and healing your mind
- ✔ Acquiring some new skills in managing your mind and behaviour
- ✔ Helping yourself to grow and develop

All of the information from CBT, plus that generated by your own real-world experiments and experiences, is a lot for your brain to remember, especially while it's busy helping you to go through change. The most straightforward response to this potential overload is to write down what you learn! The kinds of things you may choose to record are:

- ✔ Observations about your own thoughts, beliefs and mental activities, and the emotions that are triggered by them, so that you can consider making them targets for change.
- ✔ Key points that you are learning from going through the process of using CBT.

✔ Notes and learning points that have arisen from your observations of and interactions with other people that may help you to change. An example may be the way a person coped with a particular problem, or an attitude they possess that you think may help you to become more balanced in your range of responses.

✔ 'Data' from your behavioural experiments designed to help test key thoughts and theories.

✔ Plans for future experiments or activities to further your growth and recovery.

✔ Notes from other books or from therapy sessions. Use this journal to help consolidate all that you are learning in one place, so that you can return to it when you need to.

Feeling what to write

You can use the 'writing and reflecting' space in the book (indicated by the icon) to help process and track your feelings. Rather than keeping a diary full of to-do's and appointments you can use the space to write your thoughts and feelings. Writing things down has been proven by research to help people cope better with painful emotions.

Imagine that you are disclosing how you feel to an utterly trusted and non-judgmental person, and that the pages are a safe place to share your most personal inner experiences. Writing can help make your personal reflections more productive. It can also help you to limit to a few minutes a day how long you self-focus on your feelings and thoughts, so that you can keep 'out of your mind' and focused on the outside world for the majority of the rest of the day.

Working through the 12 weeks

Each day over the 12 weeks outlined in the book aims to guide you through constructive self-help. Most days will have either a key point for you to consider or a short exercise to complete. We hope you will find the points and exercises of value, but more importantly we hope that your commitment to CBT over the next 12 weeks really helps you achieve your goals for your psychological wellbeing.

We hope this book will help you to:

- ✔ Set aside some time each day to focus upon your CBT.

- ✔ Get in the habit of writing down things about your emotional health, just as you would for any other important project.

- ✔ Plan for change, put the plan to the test, and step back to review the results.

- ✔ Persevere and see change as a matter of repeated practice that is best taken step by step, one day at a time.

- ✔ Record your progress.

- ✔ Brainstorm solutions to any obstacles that arise along the road to recovery.

We also strongly encourage you to recruit some support, whether it's a therapist who can act like a coach, or friends or family members who can be your cheerleaders. Think of yourself as an athlete embarking on some serious 'brain training' and ask other people to give you a bit of support. Having an emotional problem is extremely common, affecting at least half of us to some degree or another during the course of our lives. Sharing your problem with someone can be very liberating in its own right. If the other person can't understand, that's their problem; move on and find someone who can. Chances are most people will either have had some form of emotional problem themselves or will know someone close to them who has.

Monitoring your progress

Keeping an eye on your progress as you go through therapy is a central component of CBT. Keeping a record can be rewarding, because you see your symptoms improve. Also, CBT therapists don't assume that particular techniques are going to be one hundred per cent effective, one hundred per cent of the time. Therapy is like life – an experiment. If you notice that your problems are not improving after the first few weeks (and it often can take four to six weeks to see results), it may be useful to step back and consider whether you need to introduce a different amount or type of change.

At the end of each week of the 12 weeks, this journal invites you to record your progress using the chart shown in Table 1. You'll notice that there are three major emotional states to rate from 0 (meaning that this is not a problem) to 10, the worst you can possibly imagine a person may ever feel. Be careful not to let any 'all or nothing thinking' drag you into rating symptoms at the extreme ends of the scale if, in fact, you feel better or worse. You need a good, straight yardstick against which to measure your change.

The two rows marked *personalised measure* in the table are for key examples of your emotions or behaviours, that you feel represent your problems, and would provide a good measure of your personal change. A personalised measure might be an emotion we haven't listed (hurt, jealousy or shame, for example) or it might be a behaviour such as avoidance of something, spending too much time in bed, excessively checking something, worrying or ruminating, and so on. The key is to focus upon what might be a useful measure of improving psychological health for you as an individual. Keep the same personalised measures throughout the 12 weeks,

What would you consider those key emotions or behaviors to be? Please write them down here:

1. _____

2. _____

Table 1: Rating Your Symptoms

Anxiety or nervousness	0-10
Depression or sadness	0-10
Anger or irritability	0-10
Personalised measure 1 (please write here)	0-10
Personalised measure 2 (please write here)	0-10

Remember to use a scale in which

  0 = No problem at all

  10 = Very severe and extreme problem

Your turn: Starting on your plan for recovery

What follows is some free space for you start out on your journey towards improving your emotional health, by writing out your initial plan. This book (probably alongside working with a therapist or using other self-help resources) will help you to think about this further, but to start:

What would you like CBT to help you achieve over the next twelve weeks?

_____

_____

_____

_____

_____

_____

_____

_____

_____

_____

_____

_____

_____

What is your gut feeling about what you need to change about yourself, your lifestyle or your circumstances to achieve the differences you've written about above?

What obstacles can you foresee to making these changes, and how do you plan to overcome them?

_____

_____

_____

_____

_____

_____

_____

_____

_____

_____

_____

_____

_____

_____

_____

_____

_____

_____

Part II
Twelve Weeks of CBT

The 5th Wave   By Rich Tennant

"This journal says I should write down three things I'm grateful for."

In this part . . .

Here's where you'll find the real meat of *CBT Journal For Dummies*. This part contains a wealth of exercises, advice and guidance, all aimed at helping you along the way with your CBT practice. There's also a stack of space in which you can record your own thoughts, ideas and feelings, as well as a number of checkpoints you can use to record your progress.

Twelve Weeks of CBT

. . . .

*T*he section that follows is mostly space in which you can plan for change, try out some techniques, write down your thoughts and feelings, and record your progress. This book is designed to be your companion through twelve weeks of commitment to change, healing, and growth. We hope you will take up the opportunity and use this book to help you stay on course. It's one thing to decide to change; it's another to keep renewing that commitment day after day until you recover or achieve your goals.

The blank space in this book is in many ways far more important than the ideas, exercises and quotes we have put in. Doctors and lawyers say that 'if it isn't written down, it didn't happen'; the point is that each day, valuable experiences and information just pass us by. We simply can't take it all in and remember it, and our thinking biases can mean that we miss what's important to help us grow and develop.

Over the next twelve weeks, we hope that you will use this book as your central record of all that relates to improving your psychological health. This is *your* journal – use it in any way that will help you make the most of the next twelve weeks of change. If any of the exercises or techniques in the following 'days' section don't seem relevant to you, at least at a certain point in time, please feel free to ignore them (and perhaps come back to them at a later date). Do jot down what you did each day to move towards improving your psychological heath, though.

What you write might be related to the content of this book, or it might be your own personal observations and plans; it might be ideas or inspiration you've gained from other people, or notes and 'homework' from a therapist. We've left larger amounts of 'free' space at the end of each week for you to use for anything you might find useful. As well as writing your personal reflections, you can paste in text or pictures from the Internet or magazines, or photographs. You can even add your own doodles (a highly underrated form of conveying information!). As long as it helps to inspire and encourage change, helps you to remember key points, or acts as a record of your progress, it all belongs in here. Like so many things, you'll get more out of this book if you put more in!

With focus, practice, and some guidance, remarkable change is possible. But don't take our word for it – see for yourself, by really committing to change over the next few weeks.

YOUR TURN

Day 1

Putting Your Finger on Problems

●●

*N*one of us have perfect mental health, and even if you think you don't have significant difficulties, consider what areas of your mind may benefit from a bit of attention to help sustain your mental health.

This is a moment to keep things simple. Just make a list of the main problems you want to tackle using CBT. Draw up your list on the next page. Don't worry if the list only has one item. If you feel you have many problems, write down up to four of the main ones you want to target for change. Make your problem list as specific as possible. Consider:

- ✔ *What* the main emotion is (anxiety, depression, jealousy, or hurt, for example).

- ✔ *Where, when,* or *with whom,* the problem arises.

- ✔ *What* you tend to do when the problem is triggered.

For example: 'Feeling anxious when I'm in social situations, I tend to monitor what I'm doing/saying and to try and avoid speaking to people I don't really know.'

Write out your problem list here:

_____

_____

_____

_____

_____

_____

_____

_____

_____

_____

_____

_____

_____

_____

_____

_____

It's not that I'm so smart, it's just that I stay with problems longer.

Albert Einstein, physicist

Day 2

Going for Goals

● ●

*M*aking your personal development and growth goal-directed will help keep you on track, and give you a clearer point of reference for measuring your progress.

For each of the problems you listed for the previous day in this book, decide how you would like to be different. Use the acronym *SPORT* to help you define goals. SPORT goals are:

- ✔ **Specific**: Covering how you want to feel and act.

- ✔ **Positive:** Providing an improvement in your emotional health and functioning, rather than avoidance of emotion.

- ✔ **Observable**: If impartial observers were watching, what difference would they see?

- ✔ **Realistic:** Causing a change within your influence, usually in yourself rather than the rest of the world.

- ✔ **Time-focused:** A rough timeframe in which you would hope to achieve your goal.

For example, a SPORT goal might be 'Despite feeling nervous about meeting people, to throw myself into social situations and keep my focus on what's going on around me, not on myself.'

Draw up a list of your goals here.

_____

_____

_____

_____

_____

_____

_____

_____

_____

_____

_____

_____

_____

_____

_____

_____

_____

_____

_____

> *You are never too old to set another goal or to dream a new dream.*
>
> C.S. Lewis, author

Day 3

Keeping Count

· ·

*O*ne of the simplest ways of starting to tackle a problem is to start to record the frequency and duration of certain elements of that problem. This helps to build a clearer picture of your problem, give you a measure of progress; and help inspire you to cut down on key behaviours as you begin to want to see the frequency or duration of the problem reduce.

Taking note of time

Try noting how long you spend thinking, worrying, or ruminating about certain problems,. Note the duration of activities related to the problem, such as how long you spend washing your hands, on the internet, or watching TV.

Focusing on frequency

Other problems lend themselves to recording how often you carry out an action related to your problem, such as seeking reassurance or drinking alcohol. You can use a tally mark on paper, or even buy a tally-counter (search the internet, there's lots about) to keep a track of the frequency with which you carry out the action.

Use this journal to keep a record of the frequency and duration of your problem behaviours and enjoy seeing the numbers come down as you progress.

YOUR TURN

_____

_____

_____

_____

_____

_____

_____

_____

_____

_____

_____

_____

_____

_____

_____

_____

_____

And when is there time to remember, to sift, to weigh, to estimate, to total?

Tillie Olsen, novelist

Day 4

Looking at Your Problem in Your Mind's Eye

● ●

*P*eople say that a picture paints a thousand words, and research is pointing CBT therapists towards using techniques that involve imagination.

Try this:

1. Close your eyes and focus upon the main problem that you are trying to solve at the present time.

2. Focus on how you feel about this problem, including where you feel any sensations in your body.

3. Call to mind an image that represents your problem.

4. On the next page, jot down a brief description of the image, or even draw a sketch. If you could give the image a name, what would you call it?

You can now look at your problem separately from the rest of you as a person.

Jot down a brief description of the image that represents your problem, or even draw a sketch.

_____

_____

_____

_____

_____

_____

_____

_____

_____

_____

_____

_____

_____

_____

_____

_____

_____

I shut my eyes in order to see.

Paul Gauguin, painter

Day 5

Looking at Your Goal in Your Mind's Eye

● ●

*A*gain we're suggesting that you use imagery to help get your mind in the right mode.

1. Close your eyes and focus upon the main goal that you are trying to reach at the present time.

2. Focus on how you feel about this goal, including where you feel any sensations in your body.

3. Call to mind an image that represents your goal. If you were to give the image a name, what would it be?

4. On the next page, jot down a brief description of the image, or even draw a sketch.

5. Use the image to focus upon while working towards your goal.

_____

_____

_____

_____

_____

_____

Jot down a brief description of the image for your goal, or even draw a sketch

_____

_____

_____

_____

_____

_____

_____

_____

_____

_____

_____

_____

_____

_____

_____

_____

_____

> *You see things; and you say, 'Why?' But I dream things that never were and I say, 'Why not?'*
>
> George Bernard Shaw, critic and writer

Understanding When the Solution Is the Problem

● ●

*H*uman beings are usually already trying their best to overcome their emotional problems. The problem is that, unsurprisingly, we don't always know how. Identifying the solutions or coping strategies that may be making the problem worse is key in freeing yourself from a major emotional problem. Often these 'strategies' have the quality of aiming to avoid your emotions or bring them under control.

Under each of the headings on the next page, list examples of strategies you use to bring your emotions under control. Refer back to the 'Assessing your Action' section in the Introduction of this book for some examples of the kinds of mental and behavioural strategies to look out for.

_____

_____

_____

_____

_____

_____

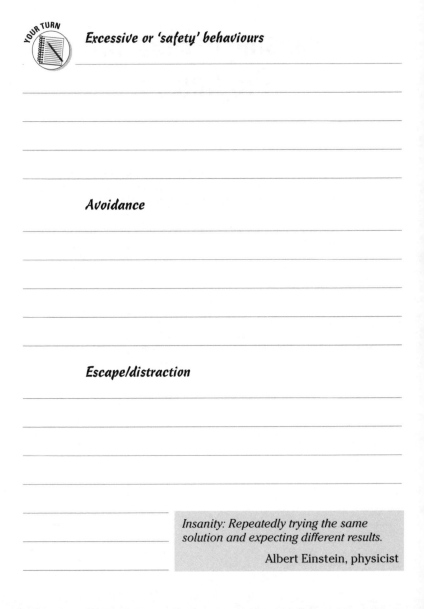

Excessive or 'safety' behaviours

_____

_____

_____

_____

Avoidance

_____

_____

_____

_____

Escape/distraction

_____

_____

_____

_____

> *Insanity: Repeatedly trying the same solution and expecting different results.*
>
> Albert Einstein, physicist

Pausing to Measure Progress: 1

• •

*T*his is a chance to step back and measure your progress so far. Use a scale in which 0 = no problem at all in this area and 10 = a very severe problem

Looking back over the past week how have the following been?

Anxiety or nervousness	0-10	
Depression or sadness	0-10	
Anger or irritability	0-10	
Personalised measure 1 (please write here)	0-10	
Personalised measure 2 (please write here)	0-10	

What's the most helpful thing you've learned this week?

_____

_____

_____

_____

_____

_____

_____

_____

_____

_____

Use the rest of the space on the next few pages to write down your reflections on the week, with an emphasis on how you've been feeling emotionally. Or use it for anything else therapeutic!

> *We all want progress, but if you're on the wrong road, progress means doing an about-turn and walking back to the right road; in that case, the man who turns back soonest is the most progressive.*
>
> C. S. Lewis, author

WRITING & REFLECTING

WRITING & REFLECTING

WRITING & REFLECTING

WRITING & REFLECTING

Day 8
Entertaining Emotional Responsibility

● ●

*T*aking a full measure of responsibility for your psychological well-being and for solving emotional problems is enormously empowering. The problem is that many people confuse taking personal emotional responsibility with being to blame for causing their emotional problems, or being weak for not being able to snap out of them.

Even if, through no fault of your own, you'd been hit by a car and badly injured, you would still need to take responsibility, to some degree, for your recovery. You may well have to carry out regular exercises as part of a physical rehabilitation regime. Training your brain is very much like training your body, and even if the training is needed through no fault of your own, no one can do the training for you!

YOUR TURN

_We teach people that they upset
themselves. We can't change the past,
so we change how people are thinking,
feeling and behaving today._

Albert Ellis, psychologist

Day 9

Making More of Music

• •

*M*usic therapy has been around for ages, but music can be used within CBT as a tool in overcoming emotional problems. To help you use music to move forward, try the following:

1. **Choose a song or track that represents the problem you are trying to solve.**

2. **Now choose a song or track that represents how you would like to be different in terms of your thoughts, feelings or behaviour. Pay attention to inspiring or helpful images that come to mind.**

3. **Build a playlist of, say, five or six tracks that help you to feel inspired and determined. Choose music that reminds you of happier times.**

4. **Listen to your playlist daily for the next week, and focus on changing in the way you want to.**

5. **Now pick one song or piece of music that can become your 'soundtrack to change'. You can use this track to motivate yourself when you have a difficult task as part of your self-help.**

Throw out rules about what's 'too serious' and 'too silly': From Mozart to musicals, if it gets you in the right 'mode', go for it!

WRITING & REFLECTING

Music and rhythm find their way into the secret places of the soul.

Plato, philosopher

Looking Back on Things That Have Yet to Happen

● ●

*T*oday, we suggest some more exercise for your imagination, this time with a time-traveller's perspective:

1. **Close your eyes and call to mind an image of a moment in the future in which your problem has been greatly improved. Call to mind how different you feel, including where in your body you feel different.**

2. **Imagine that you are looking back over the days, weeks or months that it has taken for you to arrive at your goal.**

3. **List below all the things you imagine you did to achieve your goal. List the obstacles you overcame and the personal strengths you used or found you had.**

4. **Consider how you can start to use those steps to take you forward now.**

YOUR TURN

*Logic will take you from A to B,
imagination will take you everywhere.*

Albert Einstein, physicist

Day 11

Homing In on Inspiration

● ●

*L*ife can be tough at times, and from time to time we all need to feel inspired to stay positive. This can be very true when you're tackling an emotional problem, which may involve changing the habits of a lifetime, taking personal risks and facing your fears.

Having an inspirational role model to call to mind can be really helpful when confronted with adversity. A role model can literally be anyone from whose book you would take a leaf, and who will inspire you on your journey through CBT. The role model may be a historical figure, a fictional character, a religious figure, a person you know, a family member or a celebrity: the sky's the limit. The main thing is that calling this person to mind helps you access a mode in which to tackle a problem.

Jot down the name (or names) of your inspirational role model(s):

_____

_____

_____

_____

_____

_____

_____

YOUR TURN

I long to speak out of the intense inspiration that comes to me from the lives of strong women.

Ruth Benedict, scientist

Day 12

Writing About the One You Love

● ●

*T*his exercise will not only help build upon your gratitude attitude, it has been demonstrated in research to increase happiness, reduce stress, and even lower cholesterol!

Think about someone you love or have great affection for. This could be a significant friend, relative or romantic partner.

Now spend the next 20 minutes writing about your affection for this person and why they have a special place in your heart. Consistent with the research on this technique, we are going to invite you to repeat this exercise twice more over the next five weeks, to help you get the best results.

_____

_____

_____

_____

_____

_____

_____

YOUR TURN

A loving heart is the beginning of all knowledge.

Thomas Carlyle, philosopher

Day 13

Beating the Bully

●●●●●●●●●●●●●●●●●●●●●●●●●●●●●●●●●●●●●●

*H*ere's a metaphor that numerous people we have worked with in therapy have reported to be really helpful.

Consider picturing as a bully a part of your mind that gives you trouble, and think of resisting its pressure to carry out an unhelpful mental or behavioural strategy as being like standing up to it. It may 'hit' you with discomfort, but persist with standing up to it and eventually it will stop bothering you.

For example, this technique can help with:

- ✔ The urge to avoid or escape
- ✔ The urge to ruminate
- ✔ The urge to carry out a compulsion
- ✔ The impulse to attack and criticise yourself
- ✔ The impulse to drink or binge

What might it help you to stand up to?

YOUR TURN

True courage is cool and calm. The bravest of men have the least of a brutal, bullying insolence, and in the very time of danger are found the most serene and free.

Lord Shaftesbury, reformer

Pausing to Measure Progress: 2

● ●

*T*his is a chance to step back and measure your progress so far. Use a scale in which 0 = no problem at all in this area and 10 = a very severe problem

Looking back over the past week how have the following been?

Anxiety or nervousness	0-10	
Depression or sadness	0-10	
Anger or irritability	0-10	
Personalised measure 1 (please write here)	0-10	
Personalised measure 2 (please write here)	0-10	

What's the most helpful thing you've learned this week?

_____

_____

_____

_____

_____

_____

_____

_____

_____

_____

_____

_____

_____

Use the rest of the space on the next few pages to write down your reflections on the week, with an emphasis on how you've been feeling emotionally. Or for anything else therapeutic!

Constant dripping hollows out a stone.

Lucretius, poet and philosopher

WRITING & REFLECTING

WRITING & REFLECTING

WRITING & REFLECTING

WRITING & REFLECTING

Catching Your Cognitions, Practising Your ABCs: 1

• •

*O*ne of the very first steps in CBT is to make the link between your thoughts and your feelings – the 'thought-feeling' link. Using the simple form below, catch your *cognition* – the stuff that goes through your mind. This will include negative automatic thoughts (or NATs), images, beliefs, and memories. The key is to try and understand the meaning that your mind is bringing to the event that results in your emotional reaction.

One of the easiest ways of keeping this concept in mind is the *ABC model*:

- ✔ **A**ctivating event (an internal or external trigger)

- ✔ **B**eliefs: Meanings, thoughts and images

- ✔ **C**onsequences: The emotional and behavioural effect. 'A' as processed via 'B'

- ✔ **A + B = C**.: The way your mind interprets and processes an event significantly affects the way you feel.

Call to mind a recent example of one of your emotional problems and try out an ABC:

Activating Event, or 'trigger' for your emotional response

_____

_____

_____

_____

_____

Beliefs, meanings thoughts and images that went through your mind

_____

_____

_____

_____

_____

Consequences in terms of emotions and behaviour

_____

_____

_____

_____

_____

> _Men are disturbed not by things, but by the view they take of things._
>
> Epictetus, philosopher

Day 16

Catching Your Cognitions, Practising Your ABCs: 2

⬤ ⬤

*C*atastrophising is jumping to a 'worst case' conclusion, taking a relatively minor negative event and imagining all sorts of disasters resulting from that one small event, as shown here:

Catastrophising

Can you think of a recent example of catastrophising in your life?

_____

_____

_____

_____

_____

_____

How strongly did you believe this thought to be true (0–100 per cent)

_____

_____

_____

What were the emotional and behavioural consequences of this thought?

_____

_____

_____

_____

_____

All-or-nothing or *black-or-white thinking* (see the next picture) is extreme thinking that can lead to extreme emotions and behaviours. People either love you or hate you, right? Something's either perfect or a disaster. You're either responsibility-free or totally to blame. Sound sensible? We hope not!

All-or-nothing or Black-and-white thinking

Can you think of a recent example of all-or-nothing thinking in your life?

_____

_____

_____

_____

_____

How strongly did you believe this thought to be true (0–100 per cent)

_____

_____

_____

What were the emotional and behavioural consequences of this thought?

_____

_____

_____

_____

_____

_____

Catching Your Cognitions, Practising Your ABCs: 3

• •

*O*ften, clients tell us after they've done something they were anxious about that the actual event wasn't half as bad as they'd predicted. Similarly when people feel depressed they can become very gloomy or hopeless about the future.

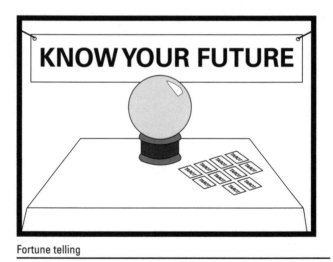

Fortune telling

Can you think of a recent example of fortune telling in your life?

_____

_____

_____

_____

_____

_____

How strongly did you believe this thought to be true (0–100 per cent)

_____

_____

_____

What were the emotional and behavioural consequences of this thought?

_____

_____

_____

_____

_____

_____

With *mind-reading* (see the figure below), the tendency is often to assume that others are thinking negative things about you, or have negative motives and intentions.

Mind-reading

Can you think of a recent example of mind reading in your life?

_____

_____

_____

_____

_____

How strongly did you believe this thought to be true (0–100 per cent)

_____

_____

_____

What were the emotional and behavioural consequences of this thought?

_____

_____

_____

_____

_____

Catching Your Cognitions, Practising Your ABCs: 4

*T*he problem with viewing your feelings as factual is that you stop looking for contradictory information – or for any additional information at all. Balance your emotional reasoning with a little more attention to the facts that support and contradict your views, as we show in the figure below. For example, buying a house – The house can feel right, but you still do a survey.

Balancing emotion and reason

Can you think of a recent example of emotional reasoning in your life?

_____

_____

_____

_____

_____

_____

How strongly did you believe this thought to be true (0–100 per cent)

_____

_____

_____

What were the emotional and behavioural consequences of this thought?

_____

_____

_____

_____

_____

_____

74

Overgeneralising is the error of drawing global conclusions from one or more events. Take a look at the figure below. Here, our stick man sees one black sheep in a flock and instantly assumes the whole flock of sheep is black. However, his overgeneralisation is inaccurate because the rest of the flock are white sheep.

Overgeneralising

Can you think of a recent example of overgeneralising in your life?

_____

_____

_____

_____

_____

_____

How strongly did you believe this thought to be true (0–100 per cent)

_____

_____

_____

What were the emotional and behavioural consequences of this thought?

_____

_____

_____

_____

_____

_____

Catching Your Cognitions, Practising Your ABCs: 5

● ●

*L*abels, and the process of labelling people and events, are everywhere. For example, people who have low self-esteem may label themselves as 'worthless', 'inferior' or 'inadequate'

Labelling

Can you think of a recent example of labelling in your life?

_____

_____

_____

_____

_____

How strongly did you believe this thought to be true
(0–100 per cent)?

_____

_____

What were the emotional and behavioural consequences
of this thought?

_____

_____

_____

_____

_____

Demands are thoughts and beliefs that contain words like 'must', 'need', 'got to' and 'have to', and are often problematic because they're extreme and rigid and they get in the way of you adapting to reality.

Demands

Can you think of a recent example of a demand in your life?

_____

_____

_____

_____

_____

How strongly did you believe this thought to be true (0–100 per cent)?

_____

_____

_____

What were the emotional and behavioural consequences of this thought?

_____

_____

_____

_____

_____

If you only ever take in information that fits with your negative thinking, you can end up reinforcing undesirable thinking habits. The fact that you don't see the positive stuff about yourself, or your experiences, doesn't mean it isn't there. This kind of thinking error is called *mental filtering*.

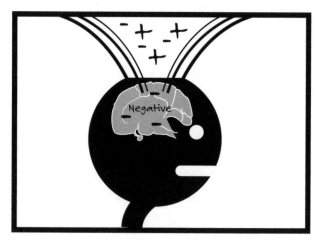

Mental filtering

Can you think of a recent example of mental filtering ?

_____

_____

_____

_____

_____

_____

How strongly did you believe this thought to be true
(0–100 per cent)?

_____

_____

_____

What were the emotional and behavioural consequences
of this thought?

_____

_____

_____

_____

_____

_____

Catching Your Cognitions, Practising Your ABCs: 6

isqualifying the positive (see the figure below) is related to the biased way that people can process information. Disqualifying the positive is a mental response to a positive event that transforms it into a neutral or negative event.

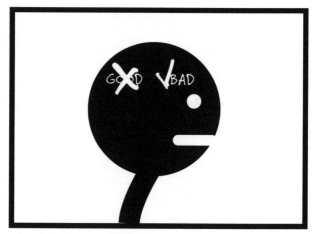

Disqualifying the positive

Can you think of a recent example of disqualifying the positive?

How strongly did you believe this thought to be true (0–100 per cent)

What were the emotional and behavioural consequences of this thought?

Low frustration tolerance refers to the error of assuming that when something is difficult to tolerate, it's intolerable. This thinking error means you magnify discomfort and don't tolerate temporary discomfort when it's in your interest to do so for longer-term benefit.

Low frustration tolerance

Can you think of a recent example of low frustration tolerance in your life?

_____

_____

_____

_____

_____

_____

How strongly did you believe this thought to be true (0–100 per cent)

_____

_____

_____

What were the emotional and behavioural consequences of this thought?

_____

_____

_____

_____

_____

_____

Personalising involves interpreting events as being related to you personally and overlooking other factors. This can lead to emotional difficulties, such as feeling hurt easily or feeling unnecessarily guilty.

Personalising

Can you think of a recent example of personalising in your life?

_____

_____

_____

_____

_____

_____

How strongly did you believe this thought to be true (0–100 per cent)

_____

_____

_____

What were the emotional and behavioural consequences of this thought?

_____

_____

_____

_____

_____

_____

Day 21

Pausing to Measure Progress: 3

● ●

*T*his is a chance to step back and measure your progress so far. Use a scale in which 0 = no problem at all in this area and 10 = a very severe problem.

Looking back over the past week, how have the following been?

Anxiety or nervousness	0-10	
Depression or sadness	0-10	
Anger or irritability	0-10	
Personalised measure 1 (please write here)	0-10	
Personalised measure 2 (please write here)	0-10	

What's the most helpful thing you've learned this week?

_____

_____

_____

_____

_____

_____

_____

_____

_____

_____

_____

_____

_____

Use the rest of the space on the next few pages to write down your reflections on the week, with an emphasis on how you've been feeling emotionally. Or for anything else therapeutic!

WRITING & REFLECTING

WRITING & REFLECTING

WRITING & REFLECTING

WRITING & REFLECTING

Day 22

Taking a Step Back from Toxic Thoughts

● ●

*A*s we learn more about how to help people over-come their emotional problems, CBT therapists have come to understand that there are alternatives to challenging and changing unhelpful thoughts.

Detached observation involves understanding that your mind has an endless flow of thoughts, images, memories, beliefs and ideas. The problem with this is that if your mood changes, the quality of these mental events can change to become more negative, catastrophic, extreme and unhelpful. You can't decide what enters your mind, only how you respond. The best bet is to allow mental events to take care of themselves. Treat them like passing traffic or leaves floating down a river, and re-focus your mind on the outside world.

Try to see each negative, self-critical, catastrophic, extreme or unhelpful thought that enters your mind as an opportunity to practise detached observation, and to then gently re-focus your attention onto the outside world in the here-and-now.

_____

_____

_____

_____

YOUR TURN

It's not a matter of letting go – you would if you could. Instead of 'letting go' we should probably say 'Let it be'.

Jon Kabat-Zinn, scientist and Mindfulness expert

Training Your Attention: 1

● ●

*W*here you focus your attention has a huge role to play in how your mind functions. Generally speaking the more internally focused your attention, the more you'll engage with unhelpful thoughts, images and bodily sensations, and thus the more likely it is that you'll experience an emotional problem.

Learning to bring your mind into the outside world and into the here and now will help bring considerable relief from stress and worry, and can help protect you from depression. With regular training, your mind can become considerably better at keeping 'out of your head'.

Today, try to notice how often you end up 'in your head' and how much this tends to be connected with feeling bad.

_____

_____

_____

_____

_____

_____

_____

_____

WRITING & REFLECTING

Do not dwell on the past, do not dream of the future, concentrate the mind on the present moment.

Buddha

Day 24

Training Your Attention: 2

● ●

*O*ur suggestion is that you really give your attention a workout over the next few days. Here is a simple attention-training exercise:

1. **Take yourself out for a walk in a situation that you don't find too stressful.**

2. **One by one, spend a minute or two focusing on each of the following:**

    - **The feeling of the ground beneath your feet**

    - **Things you can see around you**

    - **Things you can hear**

    - **Anything you can smell**

    - **The wind, sun or rain against your skin**

3. **Go back through your senses for about ten minutes then try and take in the whole environment together for another two minutes.**

    When your thoughts/attention drift off just notice and gently bring it back. With practice you'll able to stay focused longer. You can then gradually confront more challenging situations whilst practising this exercise.

YOUR TURN

Life is only available in the present moment.

Thich Nhat Hanh, author
and Zen master

Recording Your Attention Training

• •

*I*t can take at least two weeks, and often as many as four or more to notice the benefit of attention training, so this is a strategy to really persist with. With practice you should see your attention become more external and broader.

How long did you spend training your attention today?

Was your attention:

Mostly internal   Mostly external
|_____|

When you tried to take in the whole environment, all of your senses together, was your attention:

Broad and deep   Narrow
|_____|

_____

_____

_____

_____

WRITING & REFLECTING

Every artist was first an amateur.

Henry Ward Beecher, clergyman,
social reformer, abolitionist

Day 26

Experiencing Experiments: 1

●●

*I*n characterising therapy, Aaron T. Beck, the founder of cognitive therapy, emphasises the value of the scientific process of gathering evidence or data, and of putting a theory to the test.

In CBT, one of the keys to progress is to test things out. This may involve seeing whether a particular feared prediction comes true (for example, 'I'll make a fool of myself' in a social situation, or 'I'll have a heart attack' about having a panic attack away from a place of safety). It may also involve checking out whether a particular coping strategy really is as helpful as it appears (for example, 'If I don't wash my hands, my house will always feel contaminated'). The key is not to assume that your thoughts and predictions are a hundred per cent true, but to carry out experiments to put them to the test.

Start small and build up as you gain confidence.

_____

_____

_____

_____

_____

_____

YOUR TURN

*A thinker sees his own actions as
experiments and questions – as attempts
to find out something. Success and failure
are for him answers above all.*

Friedrich Nietzsche, philosopher

Day 27

Experiencing Experiments: 2

• •

*I*n many ways, CBT is the practical (and friendly) 'appliance of science'. You don't have to become a science geek – we mean treating your thoughts as theories which may or may not turn out to be realistic when put to the test. You can also use your scientific mind to check out the effects of various mental and behavioural strategies, by either boosting or reducing them.

For example, people with social phobia often find it helpful to test out the effect of boosting and reducing their safety behaviours (such as preparing and monitoring what they have to say). People with OCD often find it helpful to see the effect of checking behaviours by boosting them for a day, to see for themselves the way they increase, rather than reduce, uncertainty.

Now move on to designing some experiments for yourself. The data to gain from your experiments can be recorded within your journal writing, as you progress throughout your CBT.

_____

_____

_____

_____

_____

_____

YOUR TURN

*All life is an experiment. The more
experiments you make the better.*

Ralph Waldo Emerson, American poet

Pausing to Measure Progress: 4

● ●

*T*his is a chance to step back and measure your progress so far. Use a scale in which 0 = no problem at all in this area and 10 = a very severe problem

Looking back over the past week, how have the following been?

Anxiety or nervousness	0-10	
Depression or sadness	0-10	
Anger or irritability	0-10	
Personalised measure 1 (please write here)	0-10	
Personalised measure 2 (please write here)	0-10	

What's the most helpful thing you've learned this
week?

_____

_____

_____

_____

_____

_____

_____

_____

_____

_____

_____

_____

_____

_____

_____

_____

_____

Use this space to write down your reflections on the week, with an emphasis on how you've been feeling emotionally.

WRITING & REFLECTING

WRITING & REFLECTING

WRITING & REFLECTING

Day 29

Writing Again About the One You Love

● ●

*T*his exercise not only helps build upon your gratitude attitude, it has been demonstrated in research to increase happiness, reduce stress, and even lower cholesterol!

Once more, think about someone you love or have great affection for. This can be a significant friend, relative or romantic partner. Now spend the next 20 minutes writing about your affection for this person and why he or she has a special place in your heart. Consistent with the research on this technique, we are going to invite you to repeat this exercise once more over the next five weeks, to help you get the best results.

_____

_____

_____

_____

_____

_____

_____

_____

YOUR TURN

Day 30

Resisting Rumination

• •

*R*uminate means 'repeatedly chew over', and is particularly associated with depression. When you're ruminating, you're constantly revisiting and re-examining problems. Identifying and interrupting this mental process can have a dramatically beneficial effect upon your mood.

Identifying ruminative thoughts, and where and when you tend to have them, is a key to getting your mind back on track:

- ✔ Look out for thoughts like 'if only . . .' or 'why did X happen?' – they can keep you going around in circles.

- ✔ Become aware of when you are dwelling on the past.

- ✔ Spot where you tend to stand or sit and ruminate.

- ✔ Spot what time of day you are most likely to ruminate.

- ✔ Deliberately plan to interrupt your mind if it's ruminating, and bring your attention back to the here and now.

_____

_____

_____

_____

_____

The tricky thing about rumination is that it feels like it's helpful, but there's no action taken, and you don't move forward to some sort of solution.

Carla Grayson, psychologist

Day 31

Contemplating the Pink Elephant

● ●

*T*his is a simple and commonly used exercise to help you get to grips with the upside-down nature of 'thought suppression'.

Close your eyes and bring an image of a pink elephant into your mind. Now try really hard to push that image out of your mind; don't change it in any way, just try really hard to not think about the elephant for about 30 seconds. What most people notice is that all they can think about is the pink elephant. The moral is to treat thoughts, images and memories as passing events rather push them away – otherwise they may become more intrusive, like when you try to get an annoying song out of your mind.

You can't choose what pops into you head, only how you respond to it. The best way is to trust that your mind knows what it's doing and let it take care of itself.

_____

_____

_____

_____

_____

_____

WRITING & REFLECTING

_Knowing is not enough; we must apply.
Willing is not enough; we must do._

Johan Wolfgang von Goethe,
writer and philosopher

Getting the Gratitude Attitude

● ●

Dr Martin Seligman, founder of the positive psychology movement, has shown that deliberately practising gratitude can have a significantly positive effect on your mood.

One of Martin Seligman's key strategies to help practise gratitude is to identify someone who has helped you in your life but who you have never got around to thanking. Write a letter to the person expressing gratitude.

Another strategy is to keep a gratitude log, to practise the 'gratitude attitude'. We'll invite you add to the log each week for the next few weeks.

Write down three things that have happened this week that you are grateful for.

1._____

2._____

3._____

WRITING & REFLECTING

Gratitude is the sign of noble souls.

Aesop's Fables

Day 33

Healing with Humour

* *

*A*merican psychologist Albert Ellis often characterised human emotional problems as stemming from people taking themselves too seriously. Humour is certainly a good way of defusing this tendency. Gently poking fun at your problems can really help relieve the tension. Laughter releases feel-good hormones in your body and is really good for your mind.

Draw up a list of the sorts of things that make you laugh, or at least that have made you laugh in the past. Raid your DVD collection, CDs, books, comic strips and the Internet for something that makes you laugh at least once a day.

Try to see the absurd and humorous in every-day life, and foster your sense of humour as an important aspect of your mind.

If you're feeling depressed, it can be extremely hard to find anything funny, so at this point see thinking about what makes you laugh as simply adding variety to your diet of activity.

YOUR TURN

The best things in life are silly.

Scott Adams, creator
of cartoon strip 'Dilbert'

Calming Down Criticism

• •

*R*ecently, researchers have come to understand that many negative and critical thoughts don't just happen, but are part of a deliberate strategy on behalf of the individual. The following are some of the motivations that people have behind self-criticism:

- ✔ It's important to be self-critical to stop me becoming arrogant.

- ✔ It's important to be self-critical to stop me becoming complacent.

- ✔ It's important to be self-critical to keep up high standards.

- ✔ It's important to be self-critical so that I'm not easily caught off guard or hurt if someone else criticises me.

Do you notice any other positive beliefs that you hold about keeping up criticism? Jot them down in the space opposite.

If someone tried to sell you being self-critical as a medicine, would you buy it on the strength of its results versus its side effects? We suspect not. If you're still unsure, give self-directed kindness and compassion a good trial and see what you make of it!

YOUR TURN

Any fool can criticize, condemn, and complain but it takes character and self-control to be understanding and forgiving.

Dale Carnegie, self-improvement writer

Pausing to Measure Progress: 5

● ●

*T*his is a chance to step back and measure your progress so far. Use a scale in which 0 = no problem at all in this area and 10 = a very severe problem

Looking back over the past week how have the following been?

Anxiety or nervousness	0-10	
Depression or sadness	0-10	
Anger or irritability	0-10	
Personalised measure 1 (please write here)	0-10	
Personalised measure 2 (please write here)	0-10	

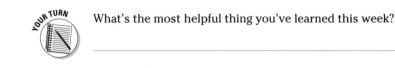 What's the most helpful thing you've learned this week?

_____

_____

_____

_____

_____

_____

_____

_____

_____

Gratitude Practice:

Write down three things that have happened this week that you are grateful for.

1._____

2._____

3._____

> *There are no constraints on the human mind, no walls around the human spirit, no barriers to our progress except those we ourselves erect.*
>
> Ronald Reagan, U.S. president

Use this space, and that on the following pages, to write down your reflections on the week, with an emphasis on how you've been feeling emotionally.

WRITING & REFLECTING

WRITING & REFLECTING

WRITING & REFLECTING

Day 36

Dealing with Decisions

*I*n personal change, decision-making is a key process. Not only do you have to decide to change, you have to decide how you're going to change, and then you'll need to repeatedly renew your decision to do things differently.

One of the simplest and most effective tools in decision making is a cost–benefit or 'pros and cons' analysis This is of course done most easily by putting a line down the middle of a piece of paper and heading one column 'pros/advantages' and the other 'cons/disadvantages'.

Consider the advantages and disadvantages of committing to change for both the short and long term, and do a separate analysis for carrying on doing the same thing, and one for the change you are considering.

There are no perfect decision makers, and no perfect decisions. Often it's simply best to make **a** decision and commit to it so that you can see how a particular option works out.

YOUR TURN

There is no more miserable human being than one in whom nothing is habitual but indecision.

William James, psychologist

Day 37

Solving Practical Problems

● ●

*P*roblem solving is an essentially simple and straightforward approach to making headway with managing daily tasks, engaging more fully with your environment, and pursuing your goals and values. There's good evidence that problem solving is very helpful in overcoming hopelessness and depression.

The steps in problem solving are:

1. Define your problem.

At the top of a sheet of paper, write down the problem you are struggling with. The kinds of problems you can use this technique for include:

- **Having a poor relationship**

- **Being socially isolated**

- **Having no interests or hobbies**

- **Being unemployed or being unhappy in your job**

- **Needing training or to further your education**

- **Not having enough money or having mounting debts**

- **Having health problems**

- **Not getting enough exercise**

2. Brainstorm solutions.

Write down on paper all the possible solutions you can think of. Ask someone else to help or bounce ideas if you need to. Consider the following to help you generate solutions:

- How you've dealt with problems in the past

- How other people have coped with similar problems

- How you imagine you'd tackle the problem if you weren't feeling depressed

- How you imagine someone else might approach the problem

- Whether the solution can be broken down into smaller steps, and how each step has to be solved

- What resources you can access for help with the problem (professionals, voluntary services, others)

3. Evaluate your solutions.

Look over your 'brainstorm' and select some of your possible solutions; then list the pros and cons of each.

4. Try a solution out.

On the basis of your list of pros and cons, choose a solution to try out.

5. Review.

Having tried out a solution, review how far your problem is resolved. Consider whether you'll need to take further steps, or possibly move on to tackling another problem.

YOUR TURN

YOUR TURN

Day 38

Committing to Compassion

* *

*T*he Dalai Lama, a huge advocate of compassion, is very probably worth listening to when it comes to the value of compassion. When scientists scanned the Dalai Lama's brain, they discovered he was the happiest of the people whose brains they had studied.

Paul Gilbert, a world expert on depression, has written extensively on the value of compassion in improving mood. One of the techniques he advocates is to imagine a 'perfect nurturer' who truly embodies the spirit of love, compassion and kindness. This person may look like a kindly grandparent, a wise monk, or even a fairy god-mother. You can choose any image that helps you take a more compassionate view of yourself.

Now write a description of what your perfect nurturer looks like, and how he or she affects the way you feel.

YOUR TURN

If you want others to be happy, practise compassion. If you want to be happy, practise compassion.

The Dalai Lama

Day 39

A Word on Willingness

• •

*N*egative emotions are often paradoxical: the more you attempt to avoid and escape from them, the worse they often become. Giving them at least temporary space in your mind and body will very likely make them less intrusive and destructive.

The key is to willingly accept emotions as part of the natural experience of life. Welcome negative emotions: think of the welcome you give them as keeping your friends close but your enemies closer. The more you do this, the faster you will be able to move on from them.

Which emotions do you tend to be most resistant to, and thus need to become more willing to accept, so that you can see the upside-down way in which our 'volume control' on our emotions tends to work?

YOUR TURN

Nothing happens to any man that he is not formed by nature to bear.

Marcus Aurelius, Roman emperor and philosopher

Day 40

Reinforcing Your Resilience

. . . .

*Y*ou may be going through the discomfort of ridding yourself of a significant emotional problem, or you may be looking to CBT to help you cope with a difficult life event. All of us will experience hardships, loss, illness and disappointment throughout our lives. The techniques in CBT can certainly help. It can also help to find an image or metaphor for coping with adversity that helps you to keep going.

Here are a few examples:

- ✔ An inspirational role-model who has coped with adversity
- ✔ An image of climbing a steep mountain
- ✔ An image of battling through the rain and wind of a heavy storm
- ✔ A rock being washed over by a river

Now write down a description of the image or metaphor you have chosen to refer to for a boost to your resilience.

YOUR TURN

When you are going through hell, keep going.

Winston Churchill,
British Prime Minister

Facing Your Fears

• •

Face

Everything

And

Recover

What are you currently avoiding because of your emotional problems? Ask most people the best way to overcome your fears, and chances are their suggestions will involve confronting what you're afraid of.

From an insect or animal in a 'simple phobia' to contamination in obsessive compulsive disorder (OCD), illness in health anxiety, revealing anxiety to others in social phobia, revealing a 'flaw' in body dysmorphic disorder (BDD), a painful memory in post-traumatic stress disorder (PTSD), and so on, confronting your fears is key.

Use the space on the right to draw up a list of opportunities you can seek out to confront your fears. Use the principle of 'challenging but not overwhelming' to guide you through this essential process in recovery. You can use approaching these 'triggers' as an opportunity to test out your predictions and practise a change in attitude or in where you focus your attention.

YOUR TURN

I must not fear. Fear is the mind-killer. Fear is the little-death that brings total obliteration. I will face my fear. I will permit it to pass over me and through me. And when it has gone past I will turn the inner eye to see its path. Where the fear has gone there will be nothing. Only I will remain.

Frank Herbert, author, in his book *Dune*

Pausing to Measure Progress: 6

● ●

*T*his is a chance to step back and measure your progress so far. Use a scale in which 0 = no problem at all in this area and 10 = a very severe problem

Looking back over the past week how have the following been?

Anxiety or nervousness	0-10	
Depression or sadness	0-10	
Anger or irritability	0-10	
Personalised measure 1 (please write here)	0-10	
Personalised measure 2 (please write here)	0-10	

 What's the most helpful thing you've learned this week?

_____

_____

_____

_____

_____

_____

_____

_____

_____

_____

_____

_____

Gratitude Practice:

Write down three things that have happened this week that you are grateful for.

1._____

2._____

3._____

Use this space, and that on the following pages, to write down your reflections on the week, with an emphasis on how you've been feeling emotionally.

_____

_____

_____

_____

_____

_____

_____

_____

_____

_____

_____

_____

_____

_____

_____

_____

_____

WRITING & REFLECTING

WRITING & REFLECTING

Day 43

Directions from Your Deathbed

• •

*T*aking the perspective of looking back on your life from your deathbed can be enlivening and liberating. It can help bring clarity in what you really want to look back on in your life from your deathbed, and help you to keep your priorities on track.

Fear of looking back and regretting a bad decision can be paralysing for some people. Interestingly, interviews with older adults have told researchers that people tend to regret things they *did* do far less than the things they *did not* do. So the most important regrets to avoid are indecision and inaction.

What would be chiselled on your headstone now? What would you like to have chiselled on your headstone in the future? What would need to change in order to make sure you'd like what your best friend says about you at your funeral?

_____

_____

_____

_____

_____

_____

YOUR TURN

No one ever said on their deathbed 'Gee I wish I'd spent more time alone with my computer'.

Danielle Berry, computer game designer

Day 44

Setting Your Signpost in Society

● ●

*T*oday consider how you might more closely follow your values in terms on the kind of member of society you would like to be. This can help guide you towards actions that bring you more satisfaction and a greater sense of connectedness with the world in which you live.

Identify your values as a member of society:

1. Are there any charities to which you would like to give more support?

2. Are there any political or social movements that you would like to be more involved with?

3. Are there any causes in your local community that you would like to back?

YOUR TURN

I truly believe that individuals can make a difference in society. Since periods of change such as the present one come so rarely in human history, it is up to each of us to make the best use of our time to help create a happier world.

The Dalai Lama

Day 45

Remembering Recreation

● ●

*E*motional problems have a nasty tendency to hijack your attention, motivation and time. Among the casualties of this can be your recreation and leisure activities, which can end up being ever more neglected. This can make your situation worse. First, it can lead to a narrowing in your range of activities and reduce the level of reward in your life, which will lower you mood. Second, it can lead to you being more likely so spend time 'in your head', increasing your likelihood of you worrying about the future or ruminating on the past.

What are you values as far as leisure and recreation are concerned? What would be 'you' in this aspect of life? Are there activities that you used to enjoy, even as a child, that you've lost track of? List your ideas below:

_____

_____

_____

_____

_____

_____

_____

_____

_____

_____

_____

_____

_____

_____

Day 46

Highlighting Your Health

● ●

*L*ooking after the body that houses your brain and transports it around helps give your mind the best possible conditions in which to heal and grow.

Consider these kinds of areas of looking after your health:

- ✔ Exercise
- ✔ Diet
- ✔ Other healthcare regimes

List ways in which you could take better care of your health.

Exercise is the great unsung hero of mental health. Aim for five sessions of exercise a week that elevate your heart rate for 30 minutes or so. This helps improve your overall mood and sense of wellbeing considerably.

_____

_____

_____

_____

_____

_____

WRITING & REFLECTING

> *To keep the body in good health is a duty . . . otherwise we shall not be able to keep our mind strong and clear.*
>
> Buddha

Day 47

Reassessing Your Relationships

• •

*H*uman beings are social animals, and are built to be connected to other human beings. *Who* you are connected to and *how* you are connected to them can make a vast difference to your quality of life.

Ponder for a moment or two what you want to be about in these key areas:

- ✔ Boyfriend/girlfriend/spouse/partner
- ✔ Friend
- ✔ Family
- ✔ Colleague

No one person can meet all of your needs. So you need a range of different relationships: different strokes from different folks.

_____

_____

_____

_____

_____

_____

YOUR TURN

Whenever you're in conflict with someone, there is one factor that can make the difference between damaging your relationship and deepening it. That factor is attitude.

William James, psychologist

Day 48

Fantasising about the Future

● ●

*T*his is an exercise for your imagination muscles, and is great at giving your mood a boost.

Imagine your own best possible future. Assume that all the things you want have worked out for you, and you have not only achieved all of your hopes and dreams, but that you have also grown and developed in all the ways you want.

Now write a description of this future (below and on the next page). Add details if you can, like sights, sounds, smells, emotions, and bodily sensations to help really bring the fantasy to life.

Write out you description of your own 'fantastic future' here:

_____

_____

_____

_____

_____

_____

_____

_____

_____

_____

_____

_____

Fantasies are more than a substitute for unpleasant reality; they are also dress rehearsals, plans. All acts performed in the world begin with imagination.

Barbara Grizzuti Harrison, writer

Pausing to Measure Progress: 7

• •

*T*his is a chance to step back and measure your progress so far. Use a scale in which 0 = no problem at all in this area and 10 = a very severe problem

Looking back over the past week, how have the following been?

Anxiety or nervousness	0-10	
Depression or sadness	0-10	
Anger or irritability	0-10	
Personalised measure 1 (please write here)	0-10	
Personalised measure 2 (please write here)	0-10	

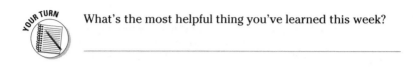 What's the most helpful thing you've learned this week?

_____

_____

_____

_____

_____

_____

_____

_____

_____

_____

_____

_____

Gratitude Practice:

Write down three things that have happened this week that you are grateful for.

1._____

2._____

3._____

Use this space, and that on the following pages, to write down your reflections on the week, with an emphasis on how you've been feeling emotionally.

_____

_____

_____

_____

_____

_____

_____

_____

_____

_____

_____

_____

_____

_____

_____

_____

_____

_____

WRITING & REFLECTING

WRITING & REFLECTING

WRITING & REFLECTING

WRITING & REFLECTING

WRITING & REFLECTING

Pinpointing the Pitfalls of Perfectionism

● ●

*P*erfectionism can really sabotage your mind and your productivity. By all means strive for excellence, but don't fall into the trap of trying harder to be a better perfectionist when your unrelenting and inflexible standards for yourself, the world, or other people aren't working.

Perfectionism can arise in a wide range of areas of your life, such as:

- ✔ **Friendships:** Feeling hurt and let down
- ✔ **Romantic relationships:** Jealousy, distress at an imperfect connection
- ✔ **Your appearance:** Preoccupied with concealing or improving appearance
- ✔ **Hobbies:** Not engaging with activities because you dislike not being great at them
- ✔ **Work:** Feeling like a fraud, never good enough
- ✔ **Education:** Avoidance or over-working

As an antidote to perfectionism consider how you might develop your less-practised skills such as spontaneity, flexibility, humour, warmth, and build a more balanced mind.

WRITING & REFLECTING

Use what talents you possess; the woods would be very silent if no birds sang except those that sang best.

Henry van Dyke, writer and minister

Day 51

Cutting Back on Comparing

● ●

*C*omparing is the royal road to feeling dissatisfied. No matter what, our brains tend to focus upon the discrepancy and draw a negative conclusion. This is another one of those mental activities to identify and avoid!

What aspects of yourself or your life do you tend to compare against those of other people or against an ideal?

Try recording the frequency with which you carry out a comparison.

As soon as you spot your mind comparing, gently re-focus your attention on the outside world, in the here and now.

_____

_____

_____

_____

_____

_____

_____

_____

YOUR TURN

When you stop comparing what is right here and now with what you wish you were, you can begin to enjoy what is.

Cheri Huber, philosopher

Day 52

Accepting Yourself

● ●

*O*ne of the best ways of understanding low self-esteem and the tendency to condemn other people is to see such judgments as a gross over-generalisation. As the big I, little i illustration below shows, everyone (you and everyone else) is made up of an enormous number of individual elements. You cannot be a *failure,* since not every bit of you has failed. A person you dislike cannot be a *bad person,* because not every element of him or her is bad. The alternative is to accept yourself and others as complex, un-rateable human beings.

```
iiiiiiiiiiiiiiiiiiiiiiiiiiiiiiiiiiiiiiiiiiiiiiiiiiiiiiiiii
iiiiiiiiiiiiiiiiiiiiiiiiiiiiiiiiiiiiiiiiiiiiiiiiiiiiiiiiii
iiiiiiiiiiiiiiiiiiiiiiiiiiiiiiiiiiiiiiiiiiiiiiiiiiiiiiiiii
              iiiiiiiiiiiiii
              iiiiiiiiiiiiii
              iiiiiiiiiiiiii
              iiiiiiiiiiiiii
              iiiiiiiiiiiiii
              iiiiiiiiiiiiii
              iiiiiiiiiiiiii
              iiiiiiiiiiiiii
              iiiiiiiiiiiiii
iiiiiiiiiiiiiiiiiiiiiiiiiiiiiiiiiiiiiiiiiiiiiiiiiiiiiiiiii
iiiiiiiiiiiiiiiiiiiiiiiiiiiiiiiiiiiiiiiiiiiiiiiiiiiiiiiiii
iiiiiiiiiiiiiiiiiiiiiiiiiiiiiiiiiiiiiiiiiiiiiiiiiiiiiiiiii
```

YOUR TURN

Its's not your job to like me – it's mine!

Byron Katie

Day 53

Summarising Your CBT So Far

● ●

*H*aving come this far in the book we hope you may have learned one or two points from the text. Far more importantly, however, we hope you've learned some things about yourself, and the best ways to tackle your problems.

Looking back over your journal, what have you learned in terms of:

- ✔ The nature of your problems?

- ✔ What makes your problems better or worse?

- ✔ The techniques or principles that you have found most helpful?

_____

_____

_____

_____

_____

_____

_____

_____

_____

YOUR TURN

Learning never exhausts the mind.

Leonardo da Vinci, artist

Day 54

Taking a Break

• •

*T*oday, as far as you are able, take a break from tackling problems, seeking change and achieving personal growth.

Instead try to rest your mind, and be good to your self, even if you can only do so for a few minutes.

_____

_____

_____

_____

_____

_____

_____

_____

_____

_____

_____

_____

WRITING & REFLECTING

Take It from Your Twin

• •

*T*his is a perspective that many people we've worked with have told us is a very helpful short cut to accessing the healthier side of their minds.

Your imaginary 'healthy' twin can become your ready reference for how to think and act in a healthier fashion. Imagine you had a twin, the same as you in every respect but not feeling anxious, depressed, angry or ashamed (and so on, depending on your main problem). What would he or she think, do or focus on in this situation? Hey presto, you've just become your own role model for emotional health!

_____

_____

_____

_____

_____

_____

_____

_____

_____

YOUR TURN

A healthy attitude is contagious but don't wait to catch it from others. Be a carrier.

Tom Stoppard, playwright

Pausing to Measure Progress: 8

● ●

*T*his is a chance to step back and measure your progress so far. Use a scale in which 0 = no problem at all in this area and 10 = a very severe problem. Looking back over the past week, how have the following been?

Anxiety or nervousness	0-10	
Depression or sadness	0-10	
Anger or irritability	0-10	
Personalised measure 1 (please write here)	0-10	
Personalised measure 2 (please write here)	0-10	

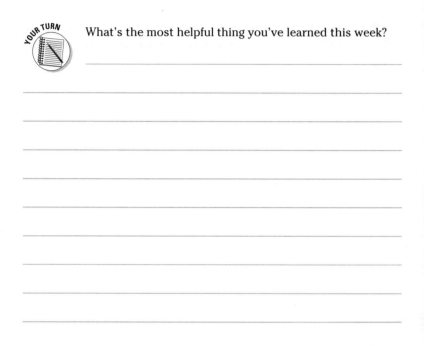

YOUR TURN What's the most helpful thing you've learned this week?

_____

_____

_____

_____

_____

_____

_____

_____

_____

Gratitude Practice:

Write down three things that have happened this week that you are grateful for.

1._____

2._____

3._____

First say to yourself what you would be: and then do what you have to do.

Epictetus, philosopher

Use this space, and that which follows, to write down your reflections on the week, with an emphasis on how you've been feeling emotionally.

_____

_____

_____

_____

_____

_____

_____

_____

_____

_____

_____

_____

_____

_____

_____

_____

_____

_____

WRITING & REFLECTING

Day 57

Withdrawing from Worry

*W*orry is an extremely common problem and can cause considerable distress and interference in a person's life. One of the keys to overcoming worry is to understand the motivations that you hold for this key mental activity. Examples of such motivations are:

- Worry helps me to be prepared for or to avoid problems.
- Things are less likely to happen if I worry about them.
- If I assume the worst, I'll be relieved if things go okay.
- Analysing problems helps me solve them or find answers.

Lies! – we've never heard anyone say 'That was a really good worry!' To make matters worse, people also often go on to worry about being worried:

- I worry myself ill, my body can't take it.
- I'll lose control of my mind with all this worry.
- My worrying may escalate out of control.

The answer to worry is to:

- Understand that worry is harmless.
- Debunk your beliefs about worry being a positive thing.
- Train yourself to engage in problem solving only when you're in the right time and place (some things simply cannot be solved or known), not in your head.
- Detach and observe thoughts about problems or doubts without responding to them.

WRITING & REFLECTING

I am an old man and have known a great many troubles, but most of them never happened.

Mark Twain, author

Finding Forgiveness

. . . .

*M*ost of us will have been wronged or let down by people in our lives, and the chances are that there is someone you are having some kind of difficulty with in your life right now.

We're going to suggest that learning to be forgiving rather than hurt, angry or resentful will make a significant positive contribution to your health. And that's the key point. Many people resist forgiving because they confuse it with somehow doing the other person a favour or letting them off the hook. The truth is that the person who stands to gain the most from your forgiveness is you! Forgiving will help you reduce negative feelings, help free your mind from ruminating and dwelling on certain thoughts, and foster compassion and understanding. It may even help strengthen your relationships.

Write down who you feel it may be helpful to be more forgiving towards, and how you would need to think about him or her to foster forgiveness.

_____

_____

_____

_____

_____

_____

YOUR TURN

'Truth is, everybody is going to hurt you; you just gotta find the ones worth suffering for.'

Bob Marley, singer/songwriter

Overcoming Obstacles

• •

*E*ncountering obstacles to your progress is perfectly normal. Nobody we've ever worked with has had a smooth and trouble-free recovery.

The kinds of obstacles people sometimes have enter their minds include:

- ✔ I can see how it could work for other people, but . . .

- ✔ If only I had a different kind of problem.

- ✔ I've tried it all before and it didn't work.

- ✔ If I do this, I may end up worse.

- ✔ I'm not sure I want to tolerate the possible discomfort.

The trick is to normalise obstacles and setbacks, and see them as opportunities to hone your CBT skills. Detach and observe negative thoughts about recovery as 'just thoughts' and see CBT as an experiment to put your reservations to the test.

List ten things you would do differently if you could be a hundred per cent sure that you could overcome your emotional problems.

_____

_____

_____

_____

_____

_____

_____

_____

_____

_____

_____

_____

_____

_____

_____

_____

_____

_____

Day 60

Perfect Recall

● ●

*T*oday, call to mind one of the best experiences of your life that you can remember – a time when you felt especially happy, contented, satisfied, moved or rewarded. A party, a great meal with friends or family, falling in love, a fantastic movie, concert, or trip to the theatre, a day out with a great friend, an incredible time with nature . . . the possibilities are endless, and we will all have at least one of these moments. Be careful not to judge or compare your experiences. It's part of your unique history, and here it's a private moment of reflection.

Now use the next page to write a description of the event. Add details if you can like sights, sounds, smells, emotions and bodily sensations to help really bring the memory to life.

One of the effects of depression is that it can make your memory overly 'generalised', meaning it can be difficult to have clear recall of a specific positive event. If you are feeling low in mood, have a go at this exercise, but do come back and do it again when your mood is brighter (the evening can be better than the morning for many people). The memory will be there, just give your mind a chance to be in a good enough place to recall it.

YOUR TURN

Memory is a way of holding on to the things you love, the things you are, the things you never want to lose.

Kevin Arnold, character in the TV show
'The Wonder Years'

Day 61

Engaging with Your Environment

One of the potential weaknesses of focusing on psychological self-help is that while you are spending time attending to your inner world, you can end up not giving enough attention to the outside world in which you live, work, study, eat and sleep. Today, consider how you might improve your environment, in the spirit of improving your emotional health.

Improving your environment may be as simple as putting a pot plant on your desk or de-cluttering your bedroom, weeding the garden, or getting on top of the bills. At the other extreme, it may involve re-furbishing your home or workspace. Try moving the furniture around in a room you spend time in; it's surprising how much it can help you take a fresh perspective.

On the next page, jot down some ideas for improving your environment by making your environment a more pleasant place to be.

Try out the pot plant for your environment, and take responsibility for looking after it. Studies have shown that this can improve your mood, reduce stress, and even increase your creativity!

A house is not a home unless it contains food and fire for the mind as well as the body.

Benjamin Franklin,
scientist and statesman

Day 62

Writing Again About the One You Love

● ●

*R*emember, this exercise not only will help build upon your gratitude attitude, it has been demonstrated in research to increase happiness, reduce stress, and even lower cholesterol!

Once more, think about someone you love or have great affection for. This could be a significant friend, relative or romantic partner. Now spend the next 20 minutes writing about your affection for this person and why they have a special place in your heart.

_____

_____

_____

_____

_____

_____

_____

_____

YOUR TURN

A loving heart is the beginning of all knowledge.

Thomas Carlyle, philospher

Pausing to Measure Progress: 9

● ●

*T*his is a chance to step back and measure your progress so far. Use a scale in which 0 = no problem at all in this area and 10 = a very severe problem

Looking back over the past week how have the following been?

Anxiety or nervousness	0-10	
Depression or sadness	0-10	
Anger or irritability	0-10	
Personalised measure 1 (please write here)	0-10	
Personalised measure 2 (please write here)	0-10	

What's the most helpful thing you've learned this week?

_____

_____

_____

_____

_____

_____

_____

_____

_____

_____

_____

Gratitude Practice:

Write down three things that have happened this week that you are grateful for.

1._____

2._____

3._____

Use this space, and that on the following pages, to write
down your reflections on the week, with an emphasis on
how you've been feeling emotionally.

_____

_____

_____

_____

_____

_____

_____

_____

_____

_____

_____

_____

_____

_____

_____

_____

_____

WRITING & REFLECTING

WRITING & REFLECTING

WRITING & REFLECTING

WRITING & REFLECTING

Day 64

Putting in Positive Data

● ●

*O*ur minds often need a lot of help in getting around their tendency to discount, ignore, and twist positive information. One of the keys to helping with this problem is to deliberately 'log' information that you would usually ignore, so as to help weaken an unhelpful belief.

Identify an extreme or unhelpful belief that you have held about yourself (for example, I'm not good enough, a failure, and so on), the world (for example, it's dangerous), or others (for example, people will put me down) for a long time that underpins your emotional problems.

_____

_____

_____

List evidence that shows that your unhelpful belief is not 100 per cent true, 100 per cent of the time. The key is to notice the small bits of evidence – the evidence is there, it's just that your mind might need some help to start noticing it. Turn the corner of this page, so that you can keep coming back to to it, adding more 'data'.

_____

_____

_____

YOUR TURN

Revisiting When the Solution Is the Problem

● ●

*A*s we've seen already, identifying the solutions or coping strategies that may be making the problem worse is key in freeing yourself from a major emotional problem.

Having progressed this far with your self-help, it may well be that you have dropped a number of unhelpful strategies, but you may have spotted some others. Jot down the behaviours that you need to target for change.

Excessive or 'safety' behaviours

_____

_____

Avoidance

_____

_____

Escape/distraction

_____

_____

WRITING & REFLECTING

Hopes, Dreams, and Hobbies

● ●

*E*motional problems love to fill a vacuum. We sincerely hope that by this stage your mind is less filled with worry, preoccupation, criticising, rumination and the like. The resting state for your mind can now become being focused on the outside world, in the present moment.

Research shows that keeping a range of hobbies and interests can help keep your mind healthy. A busy mind is like a sheepdog; it needs plenty of activity to keep it happy. And if it doesn't get it, it can misbehave.

As your mind becomes ever more free of emotional problems, what hopes, dreams or plans for activities can now follow to fill the space?

_____

_____

_____

_____

_____

_____

_____

_____

YOUR TURN

KISS: Keep It Simple, Self-helper!

● ●

*C*oming to the end of this book, you will have covered a number of techniques and committed a number of days to personal change. This means you can consider yourself a person of experience in CBT self-help. One of the things the more geeky therapists (yes, that does include us) will ask each other regarding a particular clinical problem is: 'If you were able to change only one thing with your patient, what would it be?'

So, looking back over your experience of CBT and introducing it into your life, if you were able to continue using one aspect of CBT, what would it be?

Write it down here.

_____

_____

_____

_____

We hope you'll find whichever technique or principle you've chosen helpful now and for the foreseeable future, and that you will keep on using it.

WRITING & REFLECTING

Day 68

Contemplating Certainty

● ●

*I*ntolerance of uncertainty is like giving yourself an allergic reaction to life. The only thing we can be sure of is that we'll die one day, although exactly how or when is still pretty unsure for most of us. Practising tolerance or even embracing uncertainty is a sure way to help your mental health.

A desperately thirsty camel is walking in a desert and reaches a fork in the track. He knows that down one track there is fresh drinking water, and down one track there is no water for many miles. However, he does not know which path is which. He thinks to himself, 'I must be totally certain that I choose the right path, otherwise I'll surely die!'

So what became of the camel?

He died while endlessly debating in his mind which was the right path.

Consider whether you ever end up limiting your opportunities because you think you need to be certain. If you do, try out living with a bit more doubt and free yourself from needless worry and anxiety.

WRITING & REFLECTING

> *If we insist on being as sure as is conceivable . . . we must be content to creep along the ground and can never soar.*
>
> John Henry Newman, churchman

Day 69

Experiencing Experiments: 3

· ·

*1*n the spirit of being your own cognitive therapist, check with yourself that you are staying 'scientific'. Again, by this we mean that you are treating your thoughts as theories which may or may not turn out to be realistic when put to the test. You can also use your scientific mind to check the effect of various mental and behavioural strategies by either boosting or reducing them.

What might be 'hunches', predictions or theories that you could still do with putting to the test? Are there any that would be more possible to carry out now that you've progressed?

_____

_____

_____

_____

_____

_____

_____

_____

YOUR TURN

Pausing to Measure Progress: 10

● ●

*T*his is a chance to step back and measure your progress so far. Use a scale in which 0 = no problem at all in this area and 10 = a very severe problem

Looking back over the past week, how have the following been?

Anxiety or nervousness	0-10	
Depression or sadness	0-10	
Anger or irritability	0-10	
Personalised measure 1 (please write here)	0-10	
Personalised measure 2 (please write here)	0-10	

What's the most helpful thing you've learned this week?

_____

_____

_____

_____

_____

_____

_____

Use this space to write down your reflections on the week, with an emphasis on how you've been feeling emotionally.

_____

_____

_____

_____

_____

_____

WRITING & REFLECTING

WRITING & REFLECTING

WRITING & REFLECTING

Day 71

Detaching from Your Defences

● ●

*S*elf-esteem is a curious beast. Healthy self-esteem can require a fair bit of maintenance, because it's so easy to fall into self-criticism or avoidance and compensatory strategies that you hope will help protect or boost your self-esteem.

Healthy self-esteem is an unconditional sense of being 'good enough'. It doesn't require:

- ✔ Self-attacking to keep it in check

- ✔ An inflated sense of superiority

- ✔ Comparing, competing or perfectionism

- ✔ Avoidance of accepting criticism or your fallibility

- ✔ Viewing empathy, apology, thanks or compassion as weaknesses to avoid

Write down here how you might act and think differently if you truly had a kind, compassionate and unconditional acceptance of yourself.

Now see how it works to put these differences into practice.

WRITING & REFLECTING

Putting off Procrastination

● ●

*W*aiting until the *right time* or until you *feel like it* or are in the *right frame of mind* can be one of the biggest obstacles to living productively. NOW is the time to put an end to procrastination.

Like almost everything else, procrastinating is a matter of practice. The more you do it, the more procrastination becomes second nature. Here are some points to help you get into the 'now not later' habit:

1. List five things you tend to be most likely to put off.

   _____

   _____

   _____

   _____

   _____

2. Identify how you would like to approach these differently. Be as specific and concrete as you can.

   _____

   _____

   _____

   _____

   _____

3. List the thoughts and attitudes that tend to drive your procrastination. For example:

- I'm too tired; I need to rest first.
- It'll make me feel worse.
- I couldn't bear it if I found out I can't do it.
- It'll take forever.
- It'll be too unpleasant.
- If I'm not sure I can do it properly, it's not worth doing at all.
- I need someone to help me.

_____

_____

_____

_____

_____

_____

_____

_____

_____

_____

_____

_____

_____

_____

_____

_____

4. Develop an alternative to your task-interfering thoughts, such as:

  • Maybe I'll feel more energetic once I've got going.

  • Maybe I'll feel better for having got something done or at least underway.

  • Maybe I can do it – let's see. I don't have anything to lose.

  • Things always seem worse in anticipation; let's see how long it really takes.

  • Perfectionism rarely helps! Let me stick with doing a *good enough* job. It's better to have an *actual* task done imperfectly than it is to have the ideal that exists only in my mind.

  • I'm pretty resourceful; let's try doing this myself first, and ask for help later if I still really need it.

  _____

  _____

  _____

  _____

  _____

  _____

  _____

  _____

  _____

  _____

  _____

5. Now try practising the 'just do it' philosophy in the areas you've listed. See if you can practise in as many small ways as you can to keep you in the right 'mode'.

YOUR TURN

Day 73

Aiming for Assertiveness

* * *

*T*he word 'assertiveness' can conjure up images of people in evening classes becoming ever more militant about 'not taking it lying down any more!' Luckily, skilful assertion has nothing to do with aggressively standing up for yourself at the slightest hint of rude or inappropriate behaviour. Used flexibly, with empathy and respect, assertion means becoming a clearer communicator and becoming better at saying no without feeling guilty, all in a way that is in the spirit of warmth not defensiveness.

Some of your 'rights' to hold in mind to help you assert yourself are:

- ✔ To make my own needs a priority, and limit the degree of responsibility I take for others
- ✔ To make a mistake without shame
- ✔ To change my mind
- ✔ To celebrate my successes
- ✔ To be my unique self
- ✔ To refuse requests and say no without guilt
- ✔ To ask for what I want

Write down when, where, and with whom you might be more assertive.

_____

_____

_____

_____

_____

_____

If you find your commitment to being more assertive, rather than passive, indirect, or agressive needs a boost, write down the 'pros and cons'

_____

_____

_____

_____

_____

_____

_____

Day 74

Ceasing Solving the Unsolvable

● ●

A reminder here to help you steer clear of obsessions, rumination and worry. The key is to watch out for those times when you fall into the trap of trying to solve unsolvable problems or answer unanswerable questions. Examples of this are:

- ✔ If only I hadn't (made X choice).

- ✔ Why do I feel so bad?

- ✔ What if . . . (X happens)?

- ✔ Can I know for sure?

- ✔ Why did this happen to me?

- ✔ Trying to prevent possible future catastrophes on the basis that they have popped into your mind.

- ✔ Wishing things had turned out differently.

- ✔ Trying to control what enters your mind.

The trick is to spot these unsolvable problems and unanswerable questions as being part of the problem, not the solution. Then try to avoid participating in these processes and re-focus on the here and now – the outside world.

Jot down any 'unsolvables' or 'unanswerables' you might fall into.

WRITING & REFLECTING

Day 75

Putting Your Rose-tinted Spectacles Back on

• •

*O*ne way of understanding what's happened when you've developed an emotional problem is that you've lost your rose-tinted glasses. It turns out that people without emotional problem generally have a slight bias towards the positive, even if it's not 100% realistic.

Hence steer clear of over-doing cold hard reality in your thinking, and instead try to practise a degree of healthy optimism. Your brain will thank you for it!

Each day try to find something that's open to interpretation and practise looking on the brighter side. With practice you will start to be more optimistic by nature (your rose tinted specs will have come back) and this will put far less strain on your mind, and help your emotional system recover. Your mind will actively look for what you label as important. So for example, make , people being friendly and supportive important rather than the opposite. You will see the world gradually become rosier!

WRITING & REFLECTING

Revisiting Toxic Thoughts

• •

*H*ave a quick look back at days 16–20 earlier in this book. Remind yourself of your thinking errors, if you haven't done so recently. Hopefully you will notice that you have those kinds of negative thoughts less often, for less time, and that you believe them less. Also we hope you can more readily recognise them as thoughts or images, as products of your mind rather than facts.

Most people find that they are more prone to one or two unhelpful thinking styles in particular.

From what you've learned so far, what might be the unhelpful thinking style(s) you are most prone to?

What's the effect of these on your feelings and behaviour?

Now you can go forwards with a special focus on taking these thoughts with a pinch (or possibly a bucket) of salt!

_____

_____

_____

_____

_____

_____

WRITING & REFLECTING

The happiness of your life depends upon the quality of your thoughts: therefore, guard accordingly and take care that you entertain no notions unsuitable to virtue and reasonable nature.

Marcus Aurelius, Roman Emperor
and philosopher

Pausing to Measure Progress: 11

● ●

*T*his is a chance to step back and measure your progress so far. Use a scale in which 0 = no problem at all in this area and 10 = a very severe problem

Looking back over the past week how have the following been?

Anxiety or nervousness	0-10	
Depression or sadness	0-10	
Anger or irritability	0-10	
Personalised measure 1 (please write here)	0-10	
Personalised measure 2 (please write here)	0-10	

What's the most helpful thing you've learned this week?

_____

_____

_____

_____

_____

_____

_____

Use this space, and that on the pages which follow, to write down your reflections on the week, with an emphasis on how you've been feeling emotionally.

_____

_____

_____

_____

_____

It's not what happens to you, it's how you react that matters.

Epictetus, philosopher

WRITING & REFLECTING

WRITING & REFLECTING

WRITING & REFLECTING

WRITING & REFLECTING

Being Mindful of Memories

• •

*O*ur memories make up one of the key kinds of 'mental events' that we can experience as human beings. Recent research is putting a far greater emphasis on the importance of our memories in emotional problems. Memories aren't just pictures in your head. They are a combination of images, emotions and even bodily sensations. It's no wonder they can have such a powerful effect on our emotions. The effect is made worse sometimes by the fact that our minds may jump to the conclusion that bad events are happening again. This can be especially true of memories of when we were injured, attacked (physically or verbally) or humiliated (such as being bullied or unfairly reprimanded). The problem can be that painful or emotionally charged experiences are more memorable.

The key is to become more aware of when you may be reacting (sometimes quite strongly) to a given situation, not because of the situation as such, but because of the memory that it triggers. It's helpful to remind yourself that the memory is likely to be of an experience that is the exception rather than the norm. To reduce the impact of a difficult memory, it can help to 're-process' it by writing it out and re-reading your account repeatedly. If your reaction to memories is very severe, we suggest asking your doctor for a referral for more help.

WRITING & REFLECTING

Day 79

Updating the System

- -

*B*eing human, and constantly learning throughout the course of our lives, we are bound to be influenced, to some degree, by what has happened to us. In CBT we understand that negative experiences can shape the way that we think of ourselves, the world around us, and other people. In other words our past can affect the *meanings* we carry with us and then give to current events. Sometimes these meanings about ourselves, others, and the world need to be brought 'up to date'. Our beliefs should reflect a broad range of our experiences, not the 'exceptions' that were painful or traumatic.

What is a key example of a memory of your past that you think still affects the way you think, feel, and behave now?

For example, someone may have abused your trust in the past. Now you see people as untrustworthy unless proven otherwise, leading to avoidance and anxiety or depression.

What has been the meaning of that event?

How could you interpret that event differently now that you are older and wiser, so that it carries less pain and improves the way you respond in the here-and-now?

YOUR TURN

Day 80

Putting Information Against Prejudice

● ●

*B*elow is the 'prejudice model' which explains how we human beings do such a masterful job of maintaining unhelpful beliefs about ourselves, the world and other people in the face of overwhelming evidence. Our beliefs can act like blinkers or sunglasses that only allow certain kinds of information in, just like someone who holds a prejudice like racism or homophobia.

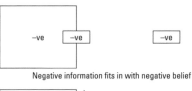

Negative information fits in with negative belief

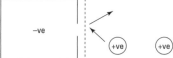

Positive information ignored or dismissed

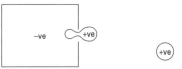

Positive information distorted to fit in with negative belief

List on the next page any observations you have about the ways you might be biased in your processing of information about yourself, the world and other people. For example, interpreting someone paying you a compliment as evidence that they feel sorry for you.

YOUR TURN

Be a first rate version of yourself, not a second rate version of someone else.

Judy Garland, actress

Day 81

Putting in Positive Data

● ●

*H*aving weakened your old unhelpful belief, it's now time to replace it! Identify a new helpful belief about yourself, the world, or others to help underpin your emotional health. Again, turn the corner of the page and keep adding to the list of 'data'.

New belief: _____

_____

_____

_____

Gather evidence that this belief is true:

_____

_____

_____

_____

_____

_____

_____

YOUR TURN

Day 82

Believing in Better

● ●

*A*ttaching your self-esteem to a 'need' for perfection is a perilous attitude, since perfection is so hard to obtain, and so easily lost. It's also often a negative, defensive, and competitive way to live. Perfectionism can lead you to consider your fellow members of the human race as competitors (it's not actually a race!) or potential critics. Not a recipe for health and happiness.

Releasing yourself from the burden of needing to make something perfect or do something perfectly, write down here the things you think it may be rather rewarding to improve upon over the course of the next few months or years.

For example you might consider developing and improving a particular skill, improving a connection with someone, starting a hobby, meditation, or any of a range of other possibilities. The art is to go for better, satisfying growth, not perfection.

WRITING & REFLECTING

Keeping up Your Connections

* *

*W*e are all fundamentally and unavoidably interconnected. This is not least because we ultimately share the same home (unless at the time of reading you are not living on planet Earth). We have evolved to be social animals, so deepening your connection with others is likely to be very rewarding to your brain, whether you tend to value connections or not!

✔ You may have fears, past hurts or pessimism that get in the way of you developing or deepening relationships, be that of the romantic variety or with friends or family. Your time and energy may have lost focus, and your relationships may have become neglected.

✔ Detach and observe any negative thoughts that interfere with your intention to nurture your connectedness to others.

✔ To help build your connections within existing relationships, don't just do the 'talking' component, but also try and engage in leisure activities together, especially something that means discovering or solving something together.

Who might you find it rewarding to be connected to and
how might you help deepen that connection?

_____

_____

_____

_____

_____

_____

_____

_____

_____

_____

_____

_____

_____

_____

_____

_____

_____

_____

Pausing to Measure Progress: 12

● ●

*T*his is a chance to step back and measure your progress so far. Use a scale in which 0 = no problem at all in this area and 10 = a very severe problem

Looking back over the past week how have the following been?

Anxiety or nervousness	0-10	
Depression or sadness	0-10	
Anger or irritability	0-10	
Personalised measure 1 (please write here)	0-10	
Personalised measure 2 (please write here)	0-10	

DATE _____

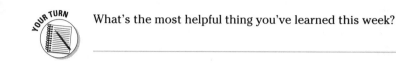 What's the most helpful thing you've learned this week?

 Use this space, and that on the pages which follow, to write down your reflections on the week, with an emphasis on how you've been feeling emotionally.

You miss 100% of the shots you don't take.

Wayne Gretzky, ice hockey player

WRITING & REFLECTING

WRITING & REFLECTING

Part III

Taking Your Next Steps in CBT

The 5th Wave

By Rich Tennant

@RICHTENNANT

"William, you're aware of how important it is for me to have a good laugh now and again, right?"

In this part . . .

No amount of brilliant insight will do you much good unless you can take it forward into the future and really use it to develop good thinking habits. This part is here to help, with advice on maintaining what you've gained through everything you've done in Part II of the Journal: building up your personal strengths, and developing your psychological well-being.

Taking Your Next Steps in CBT

● ●

In This Chapter

▶ Maintaining your gains

▶ Building upon your personal strengths

▶ Furthering your psychological wellbeing

● ●

*O*ne of the things all of us humans had better appreci-
ate is that we can't take our psychological health
one hundred per cent for granted. We need to look after
our minds just like we need to look after our bodies.
Hopefully, having reached this part of the book, you will
have taken considerable steps in the right direction. This
chapter is all about considering where to go from here.

Reflecting On Your Journey with CBT

As we hope you have now seen for yourself, cognitive
behavioural therapy is about changing the way you think
and behave. We hope you have experienced the way
in which your emotions are interconnected with your
thoughts and behaviours, and that by changing your
thoughts and behaviours, you brought about a change in
your emotions. We really hope you feel much better, or
at least are well on the path to feeling better in a way that
lasts you a lifetime.

Counting the changes you've made

Now is a really good time to consolidate your learning. It's extremely easy to forget all of the changes you've made. This is where your journal can really come in handy. You can now look back and review the notes you've made as you've been going through the process of personal change.

In the following list are a few examples of the kinds of changes you might have made as you've been striving to improve your psychological health. Don't worry if you have only made a few of these (real change usually isn't *that* complicated), or if what you believe are key changes aren't recorded.

- A change in behaviour such as reduced avoidance, checking, or reassurance seeking, or an increase in more healthy behaviours

- A change in thinking style, such as being less extreme and more optimistic

- A change in attitude or personal philosophy, such as being more flexible and adaptable

- Greater clarity of your personal values and how you will follow them

- A greater ability to 'detach and observe' from the 'events' in your mind and body, such as thoughts, images, and bodily sensations

- More awareness of the mental processes that take place in your mind, such as ruminating and worrying, and the thoughts you have that drive them

- Greater control over where and how you focus your attention, and over keeping 'out of your head'

- More effectiveness at helping to soothe yourself

 ✔ A greater understanding of how your experiences earlier in your life affect the way you tend to respond in the here and now

 ✔ Being less self-critical and more compassionate towards yourself

 ✔ A re-focusing of your activities so that they reduce trauma and hassle and increase personal reward

Write down below what you feel have been the most helpful changes you've made so far.

_____

_____

_____

_____

_____

_____

_____

_____

_____

_____

_____

_____

Deciding what to do next

Now that you've come to the end of this book and this phase of your recovery, growth and personal development, you may consider a number of further steps:

- ✔ Following up one or two key CBT strategies, for at least another three weeks.

- ✔ Setting yourself another period of time to keep working hard at changing

- ✔ Seeking professional CBT (if you are not already having it, of course!)

- ✔ Seeking an alternative or additional form of help such as help from a careers advisor or visiting a doctor for some medication

What problems (if any) do you feel you need to keep working at? List them below and put next to them what solution you think it is appropriate to try out. Try and do this with your self-caring budding CBT self-therapist hat on!

_____

_____

_____

_____

_____

_____

_____

_____

Keeping building up your behaviours

We hope you've come to understand that in relation to some of your old mental and physical activities *the solution WAS the problem*. In particular, the kinds of strategies that may be causing you problems are those aimed at controlling or avoiding your emotions, thoughts or bodily sensations. You will now have seen for yourself that your mind is very much like your body in that it makes good sense to take care of it and keep it in overall good shape, and to allow it to carry out most of its key functions on autopilot or 'in flow'. You will, we hope, have developed a number of far healthier mental and behavioural patterns.

With an eye on the future, now is a good time to see whether you need to build up further the strategies in the following list:

- ✔ Confronting situations that trigger anxiety, so that you reduce your fear of them

- ✔ Seeking out social contact and deepening your connection with others

- ✔ Taking good care of yourself in terms of things like personal hygiene, exercise, grooming, regular and healthy eating patterns, regular sleep patterns, and health care

- ✔ Tolerating uncertainty and keeping your perceived level of personal responsibility and risk in perspective

- ✔ Keeping 'out of your head' with your mental focus on the present moment in the outside world, here and now

- ✔ Holding a kind and compassionate attitude towards yourself

Jot down below what strategies you think you need to keep an eye on building up and maintaining.

_____

_____

_____

_____

_____

_____

_____

_____

_____

_____

Building on your strengths

One of the best ways of keeping your mind on track is to utilise the strengths you already possess. There is evidence that if you apply your personal strengths to any challenges you encounter, you will be more effective in rising to them. It's also good to focus on what you *do* have going for you and to cherish these assets more to counteract any tendency to be too self-critical.

Such personal strengths include:

✔ Creativity	✔ Generosity
✔ Ingenuity	✔ Social skills
✔ Curiosity	✔ Social intelligence
✔ Critical thinking	✔ Teamwork
✔ Open-mindedness	✔ Fairness
✔ Good judgment	✔ Capacity for forgiveness
✔ Love of learning	✔ Humility
✔ Perspective on life	✔ Prudence
✔ Wisdom	✔ Discretion
✔ Courage	✔ Self-control
✔ Perseverance	✔ Appreciation of beauty
✔ Diligence	✔ Appreciation of excellence
✔ Industriousness	✔ Gratitude
✔ Honesty	✔ Thankfulness
✔ Authenticity	✔ Hope
✔ Enthusiasm	✔ Optimism
✔ Love	✔ Playfulness
✔ Attachment	✔ Sense of humour
✔ Kindness	✔ Spirituality

All of these characteristics are legitimate. The trick is to play to your strengths *alongside* minimising any emotional problems.

What do you think are your main strengths to keep in mind?

_____

_____

_____

_____

_____

_____

_____

_____

_____

_____

Thinking about a Therapist

Deciding to take recovery or personal growth forwards using a professional therapist is a big decision for many people. The idea of opening up to a stranger who is 'a professional' can be a bit scary. One of the key things to remember is that all therapists are only human, and certainly most of them will very much want to help.

You would be teaming up with someone who hopefully has the skills and experience to add value to your existing self-help. In fact, good CBT *is* self-help, because your therapist helps and guides you towards a way of understanding and tackling your problems, which *you* then carry forwards into your life. Working with a therapist is definitely not the easier option in most respects, because it still needs to be *you* doing the training of *your* own brain.

Identifying good CBT

We are sometimes a little surprised and alarmed when we meet new clients/patients who say they've had CBT in the past, but when we enquire as to what the therapy involved it's very hard to spot the CBT. Or sometimes it's clear that the CBT techniques have been of a narrow or inappropriate type. It's worth checking that the person you see has knowledge and expertise in your particular problem area. If you are working with a therapist with relatively little experience, you might like to use a particular CBT self-help book with your therapist, to help add some guidance and more specialised expertise.

The following are some of the characteristics that go towards making good CBT. This may be food for thought if you've tried CBT before and are unsure of the quality of help you received. This list will also help guide you towards what you should be able to expect from a professionally trained therapist.

In good CBT:

> ✔ Your therapist should explain his or her theory about how your problem is maintained (a 'formulation' or 'conceptualisation') in terms of your emotions,

behaviours, physiology, thoughts and other mental processes. The formulation may also include elements of your past, how you are interacting with others, and your environment (such as your home). You will be able to judge a good formulation on the basis that it helps you to make sense of your problem, and leads logically to steps you can take to improve.

✔ Your therapist should help you clarify and work towards an agreed set of behavioural and emotional goals in terms of how you would like things to be different as a result of therapy.

✔ Your sessions should stay focused on your main problem for most of the time in most of the sessions. You might focus upon problems to resolve as therapy progresses. In general, good CBT has a constructive, 'brain training' quality.

✔ Your therapist should agree with you outside-session 'homework' tasks. Initially, homework may focus on reading education material or gathering more data on your thoughts and behaviours. Homework may well involve written exercises, attention training, using imagery (such as a compassionate figure) or listening to a specific audio track (such as for mindfulness practice). However, most good CBT will integrate these exercises with a good amount of agreed change in your behaviour (such as exposure, dropping safety behaviours and increasing your range of activities), to stop therapy from becoming too intellectualised. Actions, after all, speak louder than words.

✔ Your therapist should check out with you how you got on with your agreed outside-therapy tasks and check what you've learned from your homework.

✔ Where you and your therapist focus upon your past it should be with a clear aim of helping you cope better in the present, and should not involve discussing childhood simply hoping for emotional release or insight.

✔ Your therapist should be helping you to become your own therapist and increase your resilience and confidence in your own ability to cope.

Getting the most from your therapist

There is very often too much mystery surrounding therapy and the nature of the 'therapeutic relationship'. Your relationship with your therapist needs to be a good working alliance with common goals. The enemy in the room will be your emotional problem, and the more you and your therapist can collaborate against it the better.

Ultimately, your therapist is only a human being, and you will be able to help keep your therapy more effective if you enter into the relationship in the right spirit. The following are some thoughts on how to get the most from your cognitive behavioural therapist:

✔ Keep in the collaborative spirit of a therapeutic relationship. Help your therapist to help you. Treat your therapist like the helpful resource he or she is supposed to be.

✔ Be open and honest with your therapist and give feedback about the sessions, both positive and negative.

✔ Take a full measure of responsibility for your problems, and avoid trying to hand them over to your therapist to sort out. It's your brain; the therapist can't do the work for you.

✔ Avoid testing your therapist for levels of care, expertise, intellect and/or memory. It's not in the collaborative spirit. If you notice yourself having trouble resisting testing, raise it with your therapist for discussion.

✔ Don't put your therapist under additional pressure by trying to squeeze extra time out of the session, such as by hitting the therapist with questions as he or she wraps the session up. Tired and harassed therapists do not give their best. Make sure you're clear how long your session is supposed to be – they're often 50 minutes, but may be 30 minutes. Some doctors have been trained to deliver a key CBT intervention in less than ten minutes. On average people remember about ten to fifteen minutes of a therapy session, so it's quality not quantity of time that counts!

✔ If there are things you really want to get to in a session, raise them at the beginning of the session to be put on the 'agenda' (some therapists write this out formally, some agree it more informally).

Other Points for Getting the Best from CBT

As you continue your journey in CBT, bear the following points in mind. They really will help you get the best from your efforts.

✔ Avoid taking shortcuts or trying to make therapy quicker and easier. There's lots of research being devoted to making CBT quicker and more effective, but chances are that your attempts to avoid certain risks or discomfort are part of the problem, not part of the solution.

✔ Persist and persist until your problem gets better.

✔ Be prepared to put up with and even willingly embrace uncomfortable feelings if they are the kind of pain that will bring you gain.

✔ If it doesn't seem to be working, go back to the drawing board and review your formulation and consider whether the treatment strategies are on target.

✔ Take an active and creative role in devising your own plans for change and therapy assignments (homework). It really is the case that the more you get your brain to 'take the strain' the better.

✔ Educate friends and family on how they can best help you. Approaches may range from asking them to take a step back, to forming a large cheerleading squad.

Part IV
The Part of Tens

In this part . . .

*N*o *For Dummies* book would be complete without a Part of Tens, and this is no exception. Here's where you come to be inspired: either by others, through the work of ten of the best writers on CBT, or under your own steam, by a list of things you can do yourself to enthuse you on your CBT journey.

Ten Self-help Authors Worth Checking Out

● ●

*T*his chapter is a list of authors who have written
self-help books that we think are of sufficient quality
to be worth some of your valuable time. We've tried to
include books that will add value to this book. Many deal
more fully with specific problems and may provide more
detailed information or advice if needed. All we ask is
that you remember that self-help books don't help you.
You help you, with committed action and practice.

Windy Dryden

Windy has published more books on the subject of coun-
selling and psychotherapy than any psychotherapist
who has ever lived. His book *10 Steps to Positive Living*
(Sheldon Press) has helped numerous people, including
many trainee therapists, understand the central tenets
of rational emotive behaviour therapy (REBT). One of
his most recent publications, *Be Your Own CBT Therapist*
(McGraw-Hill), is well worth a read in the spirit of really
taking responsibility for your own CBT.

Helen Kennerly

A leading CBT therapist, Helen, in her book *Overcoming Childhood Trauma* (Robinson), has helped a huge number of our clients understand and cope better with painful childhood experiences. *Overcoming Anxiety* (Robinson) is also frequently recommended by CBT therapists.

David D. Burns

David Burns' *Feeling Good* (William Morrow) was a land-mark self-help book within the field of CBT. His follow-up *The Feeling Good Handbook* (Penguin) is recommended reading for anyone new to CBT, including trainee therapists.

Chris Williams

Chris Williams' self-help books are best known for his 'five areas' approach (covering life problems, thinking, physical symptoms, behaviour and emotions), for anxiety and depression. He has also penned a self-help book on post-natal depression. A past president of the British Association for Behavioural and Cognitive Psychotherapies, the lead body for CBT in the UK, Chris has helped bring considerable academic credibility to CBT self-help.

Jon Kabat-Zinn

Jon is best known for his work bringing mindfulness to to the practical business of helping with psychological problems. Possibly his best-known book is *Full Catastrophe*

Living (Piatkus Books); he also co-authored the excellent *The Mindful Way through Depression* (Guilford Press) with Mark Williams, John Teasdale, and Zindel Segal.

Paul Gilbert

Most strongly associated with his 'compassionate mind' approach to CBT, Paul wrote *Overcoming Depression* (Robinson) – a best-seller – and *The Compassionate Mind* (Constable), which is a great book for people who could do with learning to understand their minds better and becoming more compassionate (that'll be most of us then!).

Steven C. Hayes

Founder of acceptance and commitment therapy (ACT), Steven has written a number of books and papers on his experiential approach to behaviour change. *Get Out of Your Mind and Into Your Life* (New Harbinger, co-written with Spencer Smith) is not only a great name for a book, it is accessible and provides some helpful exercises.

David Veale

David is a consultant psychiatrist in CBT, with a particular interest in obsessional problems. He has co-authored (with Rob) several self-help books including *Overcoming Obsessive Compulsive Disorder* (Robinson), *Overcoming Body Image Problems, Including Body Dysmorphic Disorder* (Robinson) and *Overcoming Health Anxiety* (Robinson)

Robert L. Leahy

Another leader in the CBT field, Robert L. Leahy wrote *The Worry Cure: Stop Worrying and Start Living* (Piatkus Books), which contains a number of useful pointers on reducing worry and anxiety; *Beat the Blues Before They Beat You: How to Overcome Depression* (Hay House) does the same for low mood.

Rob Willson and Rhena Branch (Yes, That's Us)

Cognitive Behavioural Therapy For Dummies (Wiley) – our bestselling guide to CBT – has been a hit with individuals with emotional problems, students and mental health professionals alike. It covers a range of problems and the techniques that can be used to overcome them. *Cognitive Behavioural Therapy Workbook For Dummies* (Wiley) – a follow-up to *Cognitive Behavioural Therapy For Dummies* – has the same wide scope but is far more focused upon exercises to develop your CBT skills and overcome problems. *Boosting Self-esteem For Dummies* (Wiley) is a compendium of concepts and techniques for overcoming low self-esteem using CBT.

Ten Ideas for Inspiration

• •

*O*vercoming an emotional problem can be a tough experience. This list comprises ten good sources of inspiration that can help you keep going when you need a motivational boost. If your favourite source of inspiration isn't in this list, write about it in this journal and use it until you have overcome the adversity of your emotional problem.

Motivating Yourself via Music

Just as film soundtracks are chosen to influence our emotional reaction to different scenes (watch an action film or a sad film sequence with the sound switched off to see what we mean), you can use music to help inspire and motivate yourself, especially to tackle your fears head on or to keep going when the going gets tough. Keep a playlist or recording of your favourite inspirational music close to hand, and especially use it when you are going to tackle a problem head on.

Imagining You Have Achieved Your Goal

Imagine you are looking back, three months from now, and you have made great progress in overcoming your problems. Really develop an image of feeling considerably better; focus on how different you feel in your mind and body. Now, still imagining you are looking back, jot down the steps that you imagine you have taken to overcome your problem.

Finding an Inspirational Role Model

Real or fictional, your role model can be someone you know or someone you've never met. It may be a friend, relative, celebrity, sportsperson, scientist, musician, religious figure, historical figure, or a character in a book, film or TV programme. An inspirational role model, from whose book you would take at least a leaf or two, can be hugely effective in helping you access a sense of how to cope or approach a problem differently.

Finding Fantastic Films

Film can be very inspiring with its mix of words, characters, stories, images and music.

One example of an inspirational film is *Touching the Void*. This 2003 drama documentary film (made by Film Four) tells the story of Joe Simpson, who survives the ordeal of falling from a mountain during a climb and breaking his leg. Assumed to be dead, he spends days crawling back to base camp across a glacier. In extreme pain, often on the verge of giving up, Joe breaks the journey into smaller chunks; this shows a remarkable example of a human being overcoming great adversity. The film is based on the book written by Joe Simpson and published in 1988.

Other films may work as great sources of inspiration for you; if so, watch them and call to mind a key scene when you need a boost.

Listening to People Who Are Coping with Adversity

A great example of someone coping with hard times is given in Randy Pausch's last lecture: *Really Achieving Your Childhood Dreams* (www.cmu.edu/uls/journeys/ randy-pausch/index.html). This is arguably one of the most touching and inspiring videos on the net. Also available as a book or DVD, it gives a real-life example of someone dealing with the fact that he is dying of cancer, being appropriately sad about it but staying clear of self-pity or depression.

Making Your Emotional Well-being a Human Rights Issue!

Depression, anxiety, obsessions, addictions and other psychological problems can cause considerable distress and interference in a person's life. Take a look at the United Nations' Universal Declaration of Human Rights (www.un.org/en/documents/udhr) and see whether you notice that your emotional problem is acting like a tyrant or dictator and infringing your human rights. Resist, rebel and fight back!

Focusing on What's Really Important to You

When your motivation is flagging, it often means you have lost your sense of where you're heading and why it's important for you to change. Regularly remind yourself of who and what is really important to you in a range of aspects of your life, and of what you want to be about as a person. See these values as signposts in your life and follow them to keep on track. A cost–benefit analysis of carrying on as you are versus achieving specific emotional and behavioural goals can help you focus your mind. Consider the pros and cons in both the short and long term, and consider the effects for both yourself and other people. Focus on the long-term benefits. Create a scrapbook of associated pictures and ideas to aid visualising this.

Getting Started and Monitoring Your Progress

Seeing yourself improve as a consequence of taking deliberate care of your mind and dealing with your emotional problems is often the best inspiration to keep going forwards. Note the severity of up to five of your most troublesome symptoms and record the symptoms every week or two to get better feedback on how much progress you're making.

Choosing a Cheerleader

Choose someone to confide in about your problems and tell them how you intend to go about changing them. Ask this person to check with you from time to time on how things are going and to cheer you on! A friend, family member, partner or pillar of the community can all be good candidates. The key is to choose someone who is on your side and sees the sense in you applying some CBT.

Staying Out of Your Head!

Recognise the limits of reviewing or planning in your head. By all means give some of the ideas in this chapter and in the rest of this book a bit of thought, but don't abuse your brain by over-thinking, especially about things you can't change in the here and now. Give your brain the rest it needs to heal by spending most of your time with your attention focused on the here and now, on the outside world.